PHILOSOPHY IN PLAY

PHILOSOPHY IN PLAY
THREE DIALOGUES

Ermanno Bencivenga

Translated from the Italian by the Author

Hackett Publishing Company, Inc.

Indianapolis/Cambridge

Copyright © 1994 by Hackett Publishing Company, Inc.

Printed in the United States of America

99   98   97   96   95   94   1   2   3   4   5   6

Text design by Dan Kirklin

For further information, please address

Hackett Publishing Company, Inc.
P.O. Box 44937
Indianapolis, IN 46244-0937

Library of Congress Cataloging-in-Publication Data

Bencivenga, Ermanno, 1950–
    [Tre dialoghi. English]
    Philosophy in play: three dialogues/Ermanno Bencivenga.
        p.   cm.
    ISBN 0-87220-238-0 (alk. paper).   ISBN 0-87220-237-2 (pbk.: alk. paper)
    1. Philosophy.   2. Dialogues.   I. Title.
    B3613.B385T7413   1994   93-47030
    195—dc20   CIP

The paper used in this publication meets the minium requirements of
American National Standard for Information Sciences—Permanence of Paper
for Printed Library Materials, ANSI Z39.48-1984.

Contents

To Massimo and Beppe,
and to the catnip days

Preface

Umberto Eco said that there are things one cannot theorize about, but only narrate. I would agree, and add that there are things one cannot even narrate but only discuss, each participant assuming the burden of his own history and point of view, acknowledging their partiality but still defending them with determination and—why not?—with conviction. All the most important things I have studied so far seem to be of this kind: if there is truth in them it is never to be heard in one voice but only in the general pandemonium of voices desperately trying to overcome and cancel each other, and meanwhile working to constitute an experience no one wanted but everyone is happy to live.

Writing dialogues is not a perverse way of incorporating the dialogical nature of philosophy—and possibly of life—by transforming it into my own story. It is rather an attempt to get the reader involved in experiences of this kind, beginning from the hints I offer but, I hope, developing well beyond my hints. I have often lived such involvements, I have been grateful to all the participants for the vigor with which they played their roles, and I have become convinced that this is the most lively, most valid aspect of doing philosophy, the one that causes most to begin and to continue to do it. But the public is not exposed to this aspect; in public philosophers usually present themselves in a serious, formal way, acting as experts, furrowing their brows, and offering none of the excitement, of the intense, sensual taste that feeds their research. This is wrong, morally wrong: everyone has a right to this excitement, to this taste, to this play.

Inevitably, my philosophical dialogues soon turned into a dialogue on philosophy. This strange activity always made me think of a story I read as a boy, of a scientist who locked a chimpanzee in a room with a thousand toys available, and then peeped through the keyhole to see what the ape was doing: all he saw was an eye. In the same way, philosophers can do nothing else, in the end, but inquire about philosophy; after all, for them this means inquiring about themselves, that is, doing philosophy. And inevitably, since I wrote the dialogues, this inquiry touches on themes that occupied me for years, and theses I happened to propose and defend. But, for just this once, I ask leave not to take sides. However delusive one's image of oneself may be, however pathetic it may be to insist that one does what one intends to do, this insistence and that image, too, are part of the game. So let me say that Angelo, Bertoldo, Corrado, Clarissa, and Carletto are people that may have begun to live inside of me but are independent by now. Sometimes I admire them, at other times I find them irritating, but most often, and to my great advantage, I talk with them.

I thank Paul Coppock for his painstaking and precious editorial work on the first draft of my translation.

E.B.

Irvine, November 1993

Know ye, now, Bulkington? Glimpses do ye
seem to see of that mortally intolerable truth;
that all deep, earnest thinking is but the
intrepid effort of the soul to keep the open
independence of her sea; while the wildest
winds of heaven and earth conspire to cast her
on the treacherous, slavish shore?

Herman Melville, *Moby-Dick,* ch. 23

PHILOSOPHY IN PLAY

Corrado

CORRADO: Look who's here, Bertoldo: our wool-gatherer, our smart-ass, our freeloader.

ANGELO: You never quit corrupting the youth, Corrado. With all these ready-made epithets falling from the heights of your luminous forehead and your academic chair, it is all too easy to silence your opponents.

C: What youth are you talking about? What corruption? What opponents? How can you claim that there are youth to be corrupted? How can you claim that here, before us, is our brave Bertoldo, student of great acuity and even greater diligence, and not merely an "intentional" creature, a mirage to fill your eager eyes—eager for wisdom, I mean?

BERTOLDO: Are you saying, Corrado, that Angelo is still playing with these Cartesian ghosts, these dreamy, crazy deliriums, that he's not yet been able to put aside his metaphysical concerns in favor of robust common sense?

C: That's right. You have here before you one of those intellectuals Aristophanes laughed about, one of those sophists who want to convince you that black is white and white is black, and meanwhile look around and see whether by any chance there is money to pocket.

A: If I didn't know that you're always kidding, Corrado, I might take offense. But you're the last person who would doubt my honesty.

1

C: Sure I'm kidding. But remember: *castigat ridendo mores*. Yours isn't small-time dishonesty, like a pickpocket's, and certainly it's not voluntary. But if you have the guts to ask yourself in whose interest your doubts and subtleties work, who benefits when you argue that the tables and chairs around us are nothing but interpretations, readings of certain data, and readings that could well be turned around, reversed, without there being anything "absolutely" wrong with it, well, then you can't deny that there's only one category of people who are better off for it: the scoundrels who have power and want to keep everybody else under control.

B: This connection between metaphysics and power is quite popular, Corrado. Still, I'd like to hear you expound it once more, in a specific case. It would help me a lot. So how does Angelo here work in the interest of the powers that be?

C: But it's obvious, my friend, and I'm surprised that you can't see it by yourself. Suppose the farmhand goes to the landowner and says: "My life is shitty: working and sweating all day for a few cents. And all the while you amuse yourself, enjoying the fruit of my labor. It's not right. I want my part of happiness too." It's a clear, simple, and direct kind of talk, and probably one that many would find convincing. But now ask yourself: Where does this kind of talk get its strength? *What* makes it convincing? Answer: the fact that everything the farmhand refers to—his labor, his work, his miserable pay, as well as the landowner's blissful existence—all this, in sum, is usually considered *an objective reality*, which one must come to terms with, sooner or later, and which one is sooner or later forced to recognize. Once confronted by this reality, the land-owner has only two alternatives: to accept the farmhand's requests or to defend his position. In both cases the choice is a political one, and one that involves at least investing resources, putting out some kind of effort. Maybe the first time the landowner will pull it off, maybe the second time, too, but in the long run this effort will tire him out, and there will be a chance for a redistribution of power. But now suppose Angelo comes up and says: "My dear honest man, you're going too fast. How can you say that your life is miserable, your pay is too low, your back is broken, or that this guy's life is happy and privileged? It's only one way to put it, the one you've chosen right now. But the data could be read in so many other ways, and none is truer than any other. All you can say is that *now* it *looks* to you as if things are thus and so, which doesn't mean that tomorrow they might not look different to you or that even now, just as legitimately, they couldn't look different to others. How can you prove that happiness is not breaking one's back, or that your back is truly broken, or that you have a back, or that there is a you at all?" Here, at this point the honest farmhand is completely confused, retreats in embarrassment, and returns in lockstep to his work. Question: once more, in whose interest is this kind of talk? Clearly: the landowner's, who not only continues to enjoy the fruit of other people's labor, but does so undisturbed, without wasting any precious energy. Some incomprehensible nonsense gets spoken with arrogance, and suddenly all of a slave's simple, clear, and direct requests are silenced without even dirtying one's hands.

B: But Angelo might object that all this is old-fashioned Marxism, that in the end your farmhands and landowners are myths just like the "noble savage," and that in the contemporary world, with all its different information channels intersecting, contradicting, disturbing each other . . .

C: Here you go again with information. It's like a magic word for you faddish philosophers, you little academics. Do you know what he had the nerve to tell me, this Angelo from hell? Once, when his distinctions had really driven me mad, I asked him: "But when you squeeze your girlfriend and touch her here and there, aren't you convinced, then if never else, that you are dealing with an object?" And he, without blinking, answered: "All I can say is that I'm dealing with a certain amount of information." A certain amount of information, see, and don't let me go on because it would get obscene.

B: But the thing is not so absurd, after all. One starts with the idea that a theoretical entity—say, a gene or a quark or the unconscious—is nothing but a useful abbreviation for a set of experimental results and expectations concerning these results, for a certain way of elaborating information if you will, and then step by step one realizes that between these theoretical entities and other entities whose existence is taken for granted there's only a difference in the *degree* of ontological commitment, not in the *nature* of the hypothesis. In other words, one realizes that no factual statement is entirely naive, that all have a theoretical substrate, however implicit, and hence that what is true for quarks and genes is also true for tables and chairs, to some extent, and for pretty girls, too.

C: Yes, yes, to some extent. Do you know what the problem is with all you intellectuals? That you don't have your feet on the ground, you don't notice the absurdities you end up uttering. Did you hear the one about the number of hairs? A man without hair is bald, a man with one hair is bald, and in general if a man with n hairs is bald then a man with $n + 1$ hairs is bald, too. It follows that all men are bald. Now, if someone argued like this, everyone else would laugh in his face and would immediately look for what is wrong in his reasoning. *Wrong*, you understand, for the result is absurd and hence the reasoning *must* be wrong. Whereas you shameless pathetic clowns can afford to propose exactly the same argument to prove that all objects are pure theoretical constructs, and no one proves you wrong. And you know why? Because no one *cares* to prove you wrong, because no one cares about what you do.

B: But now you're involved in a paradox yourself. How can you call *others* intellectuals and blame them for being clowns? What about you? What do you believe you're doing? If no one cares about what we do—all of us, I mean, including you—how do you justify your social status?

A: Precisely by how vehemently he criticizes the profession.

C: No cheap jokes, Angelo. And I'd like to hear you defend yourself. I'm familiar with your tactic: you say nothing, let us fight among ourselves, and then leave unscathed, quietly convinced of the correctness of your position. So drop the sarcasm and give us a bit of your wisdom.

A: To tell you the truth, I haven't been saying anything because I don't know where to start. There can't be any agreement, or even any true disagreement, in other words there can be no discussion at all, unless people at least speak the same language. And I have the impression, as indeed I always do when I talk about this sort of thing with you, that we just don't understand each other—not because of bad will on your part or mine, mind you—and whatever one says the other systematically misconstrues. Thus it's not my position you're attacking, but what you *think* is my position, what you've pieced together of my position on the basis of *your* understanding of my words, which is not mine. As a matter of fact, I believe that I, too, would attack what you understand as my position, perhaps for the same reasons as you.

C: Thank you for your magnanimity, Angelo. You put it very elegantly, as usual, and offer everybody a way out. This symmetry of yours, for instance: I don't understand you, you don't understand me, we don't speak the same language, what one says the other systematically misconstrues. But don't do yourself an injustice, don't be too diplomatic. We all know very well that I am the one who doesn't understand; indeed, we all know very well that only one person understands everything, his own language and that of others—a person who knows how much others misconstrue him and sees clearly into their minds. Shall we reveal the name of this miracle-worker, this gentle sage who knows everything?

B: Come on, Corrado, don't be unnecessarily polemical: let's not judge each other's intentions. Angelo didn't say what you're making him say. If I understood him correctly, he said something quite reasonable and not so very heterodox, that is, that from the fact that people use the same words it doesn't follow that they express the same meaning, and that if they don't express the same meaning there's the risk of tilting at windmills and quarreling only for its own sake.

A: Your reconstruction is accurate, Bertoldo, except that I wouldn't put it in terms of "expressing the same meaning." This phrase seems to risk the metaphysical admission of entities such as meanings, an admission I'm not ready to make.

C: What a nice song and dance! Angelo meant, your reconstruction is accurate, let's not tilt at windmills. Don't I know this guy? Don't I know where he's going? Do I have to hear the whole sermon before I reply?

B: Well, yes, if we want to be rational. After all, rationality results from an abstraction: to discuss the value of an idea, we must bracket and forget the fact that the idea was proposed by a certain person with certain weaknesses and faults, at a particular historical moment characterized by specific problems, and concentrate instead on *what* is being said, independently of who, when, where, and how it's said. So Angelo might well be a fraud and have his own dirty hidden purposes, conscious or unconscious, but this doesn't rule it out that, maybe for the wrong reasons, he could tell us something interesting.

C: But don't you realize that this is the beginning of the end, that when you say, "Let's abstract from who says something and when and concentrate on the essential," the essential is no longer there? You've already given it away, you've already lost. Even if you win a stupid argument, you've already been carried far away from those concrete interests which are all you should care about, and you've moved to the level where the other, where power wants you. Now you will waste your time and energy playing with irrelevant sophisms, and won't even consider the real problems, let alone solve them.

B: You're really obsessed with power and don't realize that, with your verbal violence, you're the one exercising the greatest power. After all, you told Angelo to defend himself, and now you won't let him speak.

C: O.K., O.K., let him speak, let him enlighten us, let him redeem us!

A: Thank you for your patience and kindliness, Corrado, but I insist that I don't know where to start. For, you see, in a way I totally agree with you: tables, chairs, girls, you, and I are objects, not *intentional* objects, not aggregates of perceptions, and certainly not hallucinations. In other words, even if you keep accusing me of being an idealist, I believe I'm not one at all, at least not in the sense in which Descartes was one at the beginning of the *Meditations*.

C: Yes, we know, yours is a *transcendental* idealism.

A: Exactly, transcendental, and what does that mean? If you look at how Kant uses the word "transcendental," you'll realize that in most cases one could replace it with "conceptual." A transcendental analysis or argument is carried out at that typically semantical level which is proper to philosophical reflection, where one doesn't inquire into what exists, what is a cause or an effect, but asks instead *what it means* to exist, or to be a cause or an effect—where one doesn't look for factual, empirical conclusions concerning how things really are, but at most for indications as to how things *can* be, *can* exist, *can* be causes or effects.

B: Just a moment, Angelo. This idea of yours that philosophy is an exploration of the logical space of possibilities, and not—not directly, at least—of the real one of facts, sounds right to me, and it agrees with what I was telling Corrado about the need to leave out all contingent limitations when we want to rise to a level of rational reflection or discussion.

C: Yes, "rise," in a moment we'll all kneel and pray.

B: O.K., if you don't like "rise," let's say "move": move, then, to a level of rational reflection. Back to the issue, now: your idea of philosophy is fine, at least to begin with, but it seems rash to conclude that this inquiry into possibility can have no empirical significance. If, for instance, we proved that something is *not* possible, wouldn't it follow that it's not *actual*, and that its negation, being necessary, *is* actual? And wouldn't these be conclusions about the real state of the world? What would prevent us from using them at the empirical level, even though we obtained them as corollaries of conceptual propositions?

A: I must agree with you—which once more confirms my embarrassment in not knowing where to start. For certainly, as you said, nothing *yet* rules out that a transcendental analysis might have factual outcomes. Kant indeed is convinced—and how could he not be?—that there are transcendental arguments that at least aimed at such outcomes; the ontological argument for the existence of God is his clearest and most common example. What complicates matters, however, is the fact that these attempts, as one discovers later in the course of inquiry, are destined to fail, and the alleged factual implications of philosophical analyses are proved delusive. But, since I can't defend my assumptions all at once, I ask you to put this matter aside and let me continue for a moment.

B: O.K.

C: Yes, O.K. Give him a hand and he'll take your whole arm.

A: So if you let me, at least for the sake of argument, locate philosophical inquiry at this semantical level, my idealism can be clearly characterized, and just as clearly distinguished from what Kant would have called empirical idealism. The empirical idealist believes that there are no objects distinct from ideas, or from sets or systems of ideas. The table before us, for example, is for him just an aggregate of mental experiences, of representations, and perhaps of beliefs and expectations, too. On this point I couldn't disagree more: for me the table is quite different from anything mental, and is not at all reducible to mental entities. It exists and it would continue to exist even if I were to dissolve into thin air, or if I had never been born.

B: I'm sorry to interrupt, but I want to make sure I understand. You seem to be saying that the table's existence is not just a pretheoretical datum that philosophy must come to terms with, but a fact that philosophy can in no way either validate or challenge, that is beyond its scope, as it were.

A: You understand perfectly. I believe that it's not for philosophy to legislate an agreement or a disagreement with ordinary beliefs or practices: to decide, for example, that the table *really* exists, or does not exist. Philosophy must leave these decisions to the everyday life of ordinary people.

C: Those who work, and support philosophers.

A. Sure, those who work. *Including* philosophers, for they, too, are not always philosophers, they, too, work and act in the empirical world. And maybe the others, too, are a little bit philosophers, and between them and the professionals there's only a difference of degree, not of substance: a difference in the amount of time and energy devoted to a certain activity.

C: Of the concept of degree you have complete mastery. Now you must learn the concept of a threshold, and then you'll realize that at a certain point the difference is no longer quantitative but becomes qualitative.

A: No doubt about it: there is a threshold beyond which it's right to call a person a philosopher rather than, say, a grocer. But that doesn't mean philosophy is his prerogative.

C: How democratic you are!

B: Now it's you guys who are doing a nice song and dance, and yelling at each other so as not to hear that in fact, where it matters, you're in perfect agreement. Corrado says that (quite properly, in his opinion) no one cares about philosophy, and you insist that philosophers have nothing to say about what the world is like. But then I ask you: Suppose that the community is convinced, for its own reasons, that there are witches, and on that basis proceeds to roast a few poor women. Should philosophers limit themselves to taking this conviction, too, as a datum and, without questioning it, simply try to understand what it means? Wouldn't it be their duty, instead, to enlighten the community about how irrational its practice is, and try to guide it in a different direction?

A: Look, Bertoldo, Wittgenstein said that you can call things what you wish, as long as you know all the facts. In the case you described, the facts, as I see it, are as follows. There's an activity that consists in stating that witches exist, and possibly justifying and defending one's statement and drawing all the relevant practical consequences, and there's another activity that consists in explaining what it means to exist or to be a witch. Though the activities are distinct, nothing prevents the same person from performing both, at different times or even at the same time; but distinguishing them allows us to be clearer and to avoid confusions. Now, if you agree that these are the facts, it's an idiosyncrasy of mine to reserve the term "philosophy" for the second activity—an idiosyncrasy justified in part by two considerations. First, this is the activity I believe I perform within my socially recognized profession of philosopher, and second, it's also the activity I consider primary in the philosophers I most admire (Kant, for instance). If you accept this terminological choice, you'll agree that a philosopher can certainly have a position on the existence of witches or whatever, and even defend it vigorously, not however as a philosopher but as a supporter of a given scientific theory or social program or religious belief or political system.

C: Which means, once more, making philosophy neutral, putting it up for sale to the highest bidder, eliminating from it all problems of moral choice, of justification, of responsibility.

A: No, Corrado, I'm not going to take this. What *I* think it means is returning the problem of a moral choice to the status of a *problem*, and of one having to do with a *choice*: returning to speaking of responsibility as of a commitment one assumes in the first person, with all the risks involved. What sort of responsible choice can one possibly make when his philosophical position implies that certain actions are *necessary*, that one can't do without them, that they are the *just* actions? Did you ever see anyone claiming to choose and do what is *unjust*? It's precisely when no transcendental argument *forces* you to adopt a certain line that the question gets interesting: then you must roll up your sleeves, become a protagonist of your own destiny, and possibly pay your dues. It's here that I would see the nobility of human action.

B: Wait a minute. Before we speak of nobility, there are still a couple of more modest things I'm not clear about. To begin with, if philosophy has no practical value, why should we do it? Aren't we wasting our time?

A: I could give you a provocative answer and say: "Why not? It's pleasant and (for some) it pays well." But, though this answer faithfully expresses my views, its provocative nature makes it useless and counterproductive. A more serious formulation could then be the following: "At the individual's level one does philosophy simply because one likes it, as one plays basketball or cards. At the community's level, philosophy's play has much the same utility as all other play: it prepares us for when we grow up, it lets us explore still unrealized possibilities, dreams judged absurd only by habit."

B: Philosophy as science fiction, then?

A: The comparison seems on target. There's something else, too, but for the moment this may be enough, since you said you had *two* perplexities.

B: Yes, and the second one is strictly connected with the first. Considering this absolute empirical conservatism of yours, this decision never to call in question, as a philosopher, any of the beliefs and practices that accompany our ordinary life—if indeed this life exists and is not itself a philosophical myth . . .

A: Sure it is, but that doesn't prevent us from using it to analyze reality, to decompose it, and hence also to understand it better.

B: O.K., O.K. So, considering the quietism (shall we call it political?) that seems to characterize your attitude, it sounds strange that, when you get to doing your job concretely, you turn into a critic, a revolutionary, and come up with doctrines little known to me but certainly able to drive Corrado mad, or with apparently absurd statements such as that your girlfriend is nothing but a certain amount of information. And I wonder, to be frank, whether, maybe unintentionally, you're not using your undeniable theoretical ability to play the genius, and ultimately derive some material advantages.

C: If there were money to pocket . . .

A: Your concern is legitimate; it goes directly to the heart of the problem and forces me to some serious self-criticism. I said earlier that provocative statements are counterproductive. Why? Because to speak in a provocative manner means to say things that may be true—or at any rate things one wishes were taken seriously—while at the same time generating negative emotional reactions, and thus not letting those things be accepted by others, by the audience. It means to hide one's hypotheses behind a joke instead of making them the object of a balanced public debate, where they could be examined, accepted, or possibly refuted. However, though I'm convinced that this attitude is unfair and a little childish, I often lapse into it. It would be interesting to ask why.

C: The time has come to move from sermon to self-analysis. The dirty linen will be washed in front of everyone, and a soul will appear in all its purity.

A: See what I mean, Bertoldo? What's the use of this kind of talk? If you think about it, it's only to hide our own insecurity. Being rejected for the wrong reasons, because our statements are deliberately (and pointlessly) unpleasant, exempts us from the risk of being rejected for reasons we might have to share, and lets us indulge in the quiet sleep of those who don't feel threatened in their integrity and possessions.

B: Do you mean that the statements that irritated Corrado so much were nothing but provocations?

A: Exactly, but notice: I'm not saying that I don't identify with those statements, that they don't express my position in some way. Still, I had to know that *the way* they expressed it would be irritating, and would deny it the rational debate that constitutes its vocation and its risk.

C: So here you are. You finally realize how much a philosophical discussion is a struggle for survival—a pitiless, cruel struggle where all means are legitimate, including sometimes a pretense of neutrality.

A: Yes, I realize it, but I also believe that it's too easy simply to admit this conflictual nature and hypostatize it as the sole, permanent, and ineluctable condition of all human relations. One risks falling into the famous Hegelian black night. I'd rather say that, even if the conflict is the starting point, there's still room for an attempt, an effort to create free areas of intervention and exchange, neutral territories where weapons can be put down for a moment and people can learn from one another, temporary truces that make it possible to see what the situation is. And the fact that aggression is never entirely suspended, not even during these truces, doesn't seem a sufficient reason for unwarranted generalizations, or for denying that there is a difference—in terms of project and intention, if you will, but terms that are of decisive importance for human action—between a theoretical debate and a barroom brawl.

B: And a provocative attitude in a theoretical debate would be a manifestation of this latent aggression?

A: Exactly, and a way of going in the direction of the brawl. But let's return to the statement Corrado criticized. It was: "All I can say is that I'm dealing with a certain amount of information." And this is dangerously close to something else I *could have said* but did *not* say, though certainly

Corrado (with good reason) judged it *equivalent* to what I said—something indeed you used a little while ago to summarize my position. That is: "My girlfriend is nothing but (is identical to) a certain amount of information." Which would unquestionably throw me into the camp of that empirical idealism I firmly intend to distinguish myself from.

B: But then what did you mean?

A: I sort of meant two things. First, that if we remain within the traditional way of thinking, the one I call, *à la* Kant, transcendental realism, then truly we're left with nothing but amounts of information, sets of representations, of ideas. Second, that if instead we adopt the viewpoint of transcendental idealism, then we *might* overcome these difficulties and find a sense for the objectivity and knowledge we're looking for. But in that case we must make the concept of information our logical starting point, and explain what it means to be an object by reference to what it means to be information, or better still to be an experience, of a certain kind.

B: You'll admit that all this is a bit obscure.

A: Yes, and to clarify it I must return to the substance of your question, that is, to the reason for the revolutionary character of my philosophical proposals, in spite of what you correctly called my empirical quietism.

C: It's the same old story: the recipe changes but the soup tastes the same.

A: Maybe, but the reason why I judged it necessary to change the recipe is that the previous one, the recipe of traditional realism, seemed to offer no hope of understanding. Let me make myself clear. When I speak of realism, I'm not referring to practical, empirical realism, on which I think we all agree. I'm referring to transcendental realism, that is, to the conceptual position that takes the notion of an object as primary, and on that basis tries to define all other notions: specifically, that of a subject, of an experience, of knowledge, and so on. A transcendental realist, in other words, is a person who, to the question what a thinking subject is—what the phrase "thinking subject" means, what it *can* refer to, not whether there are entities to which it applies, let alone what they are—will answer: "It's an *object* thus and so, with suchlike properties." And if you ask him what a representation is, he will again tell you that it's an *object* of a certain kind. And if you ask him when a representation is veridical, he will talk about the relation between the *object* that is the representation and another object that it represents. And so on: when answering any semantical question, the transcendental (or conceptual) realist will begin a brief or long journey, destined however to end with a reference to the notion of an object. It's here that he finds his logical foundation, here that he must arrive to feel at home.

B: And it's here that you criticize him, as I understand it.

A: That's right. Not that I'm the only one to do so, however, or the first. Every form of skepticism was in fact a criticism of this model, and it may be in Hume's skepticism—the natural preamble to Kant's philosophy—that the attack found its most vigorous and extreme formulation. Let's concentrate for the moment on the problem of knowledge, though the issue is entirely general, and for precision's sake let's distinguish knowledge as an activity or a global patrimony from the individual episodes constituting it. Let's agree to call every such episode a *cognitive experience*. The problem raised very incisively by Hume, more explicitly about our knowledge of causes and effects but implicitly about all forms of knowledge, may be summed up this way: What kind of entity is a cognitive experience? Where is it located in logical space? How shall we think of it, conceptualize it? A property of an object—specifically, of one of those objects called *subjects*—it can't be, since whatever the state of the subject having such an experience, this subject could be in exactly the same state and have a *non*-cognitive experience: the problem of Descartes' dreams. A relation between subject and object, then? But what relation? A relation in which the subject has a representation that *resembles* the object? But I could very well have a representation that resembles this table because at seventy-two degrees of temperature I always happen to hallucinate a table. A relation in which the subject has a representation that resembles the object *because* it is in presence of the object? Leaving aside the difficulty of explaining this "because," I could have a representation that resembles this table because in the presence of a wooden object I always happen to hallucinate a table. Or shall we say that a cognitive experience is itself an object, independent of the other object it represents and of the subject to which it "belongs"? O.K., but what makes this object a *cognitive experience*? The fact that it has certain properties or relations? And here we start all over again. As you see, this is not the concrete, empirical problem of knowing what experiences are legitimately called cognitive: whether, for instance, my perception of a green dinosaur, there in the corner, is cognitive or not. It's rather a conceptual problem, since literally I can't say *what* a cognitive experience *is*, I can't find a place for it within my thinking and reasoning schemes. It's as if something that I seem to encounter every day, and seems to have an important, decisive role in my activities, were suddenly revealed to be impossible, unexplainable.

B: It's a rather peculiar way of construing Hume, but go on.

A: Peculiar, sure; this is no small-scale history of philosophy.

C: Nothing small has currency here: large bills only.

A: Corrado, please. What I mean is that mine is a rational reconstruction, which insists not so much on the historical person of Hume as on a certain philosophical development that begins at the beginning of modern philosophy (or maybe of philosophy, period), with Descartes anyway, and culminates with Hume's destructive skepticism. With an additional consequence—one that has some historical significance. What's the most natural outcome of the conceptual bankruptcy I described? If you think about it, it's to say: "All right, then the pretense of possessing knowledge that reaches extramental objects is a delusion. The objects of knowledge are the ideas themselves." Which is exactly what Hume says: transcendental realism leads inevitably to empirical idealism.

B: And this is when the savior comes.

A: Yes, this is when Kant comes. And what does he say? Substantially, that what doesn't work is the logical space, that problems arise because of this notion of primary objects, independent of, and indifferent to, one another, such that the world could collapse all around them without having any effect on their identity (except in contingent, factual, inessential terms, say by hitting and damaging them). When you try to establish relations among these objects, specifically cognitive relations, you're always left with the impression, if you are honest . . .

C: A fundamental feature of our Angelo.

A: . . . of just throwing inconclusive words into a void, an unfillable and insatiable gap. A void and a gap that are above all—I insist—of a conceptual nature: the void and gap that must be felt when, to entities characterized with no reference to a phenomenological, experiential level, one wants to juxtapose—in a way that can only appear gratuitous, external, accidental—phenomenological and experiential determinations.

B: So the logical space must be modified.

A: Exactly. And this is an operation of revolutionary scope, so revolutionary indeed that it's difficult even to express it, for the logical space determines our language, and when the logical space changes then time is needed before a new means of expression can fit the new space—time during which the only available language is the old one, whose use can only generate systematic misunderstandings between the bearers of the old and the new conceptual schemes.

B: The misunderstandings that are so common between Corrado and you.

A: Yes, and others historically more important, too. Kant himself, for example, was blamed for his obscurity, but this obscurity is only the consequence of the unfair battle he finds himself fighting: alone, with the vision of a new reality before his eyes, and without the means for formulating and adequately communicating it.

C: A true Greek tragedy.

A: Today the situation has improved a bit, and we can be clearer concerning the nature of the "Copernican" conceptual revolution. Before we turn to this clarification, however, it might help to summarize. I believe I've given a first answer to your earlier perplexity. It's not, or maybe it's not only, exhibitionism and greed that make me adopt revolutionary stances in philosophy. To begin with, such stances were not born with me; if anything, it's surprising that in such a long time they have gone no further. But then also, more specifically, this revolution seems necessary, precisely in order to save the empirical conservatism we were talking about: precisely to avoid a philosophical challenge to our right to maintain certain "ordinary" beliefs and practices, for example the belief that we know the world (to some extent) and the practice of acting on the basis of this knowledge.

B: I'm beginning to understand. But now you must explain how the new logical space works.

A: Sure, and if you got this far it shouldn't be too difficult to do. We said that the problem, for transcendental realism, is created by the embarrassing and awkward way in which experiences fit objects, remaining external to them, without hope of capturing them in their individuality. So a fairly obvious move could be the following: instead of beginning with the concept of an object, let's begin precisely with the concept of an experience—Kant would say "representation"—and, instead of explaining what an experience is by a reference to the concept of an object, let's explain what an object is by using the concept of an experience.

B: Easily said.

A: Yes, but not at all easily done, especially because one seems always to be losing what one just acquired. For example, I've seen many make the mistake of speaking as if experiences, representations, ideas, or whatever one wants to call the new conceptual starting point, had become the new *objects*. Which is absurd: experiences may well be objects, but as such they are certainly neither the only nor the primary ones. To think like this is to fall back again into empirical idealism, and the reason is that one continues to look at things through the old scheme, and so continues to think that the foundation of the logical space should still be the object or set of objects. Whereas experiences are something else, in whose terms objects are to be characterized.

B: But aren't you playing with words when you say that experiences are not objects but some*thing* else? Aren't objects the same as things?

A: Sure I play, at the bounds of sense, possibly beyond those bounds. But why? Because I too am forced to use an inadequate language, the language of a scheme that doesn't belong to me, a language whose most general term is indeed "object," or "thing," or "entity"—all synonyms as far as I'm concerned—whereas I need a more general term that would provide me with the maneuvering room for conducting my revolution, with the extra dimension required to accomplish the transformation I'm interested in.

C: Why don't you rather just shut up, if you can't express yourself? Why do you want to add another voice, indeed another language, to the pandemonium that already exists? What's the use, if ordinary practices will be neither influenced nor justified?

A: Look, Corrado: when silence replaces the pandemonium you will be right. Then there will be only ordinary practices, and the additional confusion generated by language will disappear. Until then, however, speaking and discussing and philosophizing will themselves be part of the universe of practices, and if I shut up this will only mean that others will speak, and possibly that they will feel more confident because they're the only ones speaking.

C: Whereas you want them to know that the turf must be divided, and the loot split in half.

A: You're really something. But in a way you're right. What I don't approve of in your behavior is not so much the conclusions you reach as the fact that you reach them too soon, by unwarranted assumptions, almost out of spite.

B: So let's try to reach them slowly, Angelo, and not to wander too far away from our goal. Are there other risks involved in the operation you're talking about?

A: Sure. The one we mentioned earlier: that of thinking that explaining what an object is in terms of what an experience is will end up reducing objects to experiences, or maybe to classes or systems of experiences, precisely in the sense that an object (say, my girlfriend) is nothing but, or is identical to, such a class or system.

B: Which you deny.

A: Indeed! There is nothing farther from my position. Suppose for example that you ask me what a principal is. I start out with a long description of the school structure, and conclude by saying: "The principal is the individual who etc. etc." Now consider any principal you know; do you believe that, if you accept my explanation, you've reduced that person to a set of scholastic institutions? Not at all: the person maintains his identity and his ontological independence from the institutions. What we've been dealing with, what we've explained, and maybe even "reduced," is *his being* a principal, *the concept of* a principal: a concept that, we may assume, applies to this individual only accidentally.

C: Look, I know some principals . . .

A: I have no doubt; I know some myself. But it's only an example, and I believe you understand it.

B: So, in the same way, what you would explain or "reduce" by your transcendental idealism is what it means for an object to be an object, not the object itself.

A: Precisely, and to do so I need the maneuvering room I mentioned earlier. I need to be able to say: "An object is a . . . such that . . .," where the first gap is filled by a term more general than "object," a term with no ontological implications—because, consistently with common sense, I want such implications to begin with objects. In other words, I don't want to populate the world with new categories of existents: existents will remain the same, those—whatever they are—admitted both by everyday life and by the most sophisticated scientific research. *In order to speak of these existents in a philosophically perspicuous way*, however—specifically, in order to explain what *justifies* describing them as existents—I need to speak of something else, too, of what is *not* an existent and hence is *not* part of the world. And it's here that intentional objects come into play.

B: You mean that for you intentional objects are only a manner of speaking?

A: In a way, yes, but a trivial way, one that might sound significant only to those who are still conditioned by the old style of thinking. For intentional objects are not objects, that is, are not objects *tout court*: they are something else, a wider category within which we will later identify objects *tout court*, the only objects that really *are*. Now for a realist such a category must be a source of puzzlement, because for him objects are the starting point, what everything else must be brought back to. So for him there are only two possibilities, if he wants to speak of intentional objects. Either he will widen his "foundational" universe of objects and say that all intentional objects are legitimate members of it, and existence is a property that may or may not apply to them and hence discriminates among them—just like being red or being square. Or he will conclude that intentional objects are in some sense delusive, that they must be reduced or eliminated—that is, in the last analysis, explained without residue in terms of objects proper. If he takes the first course, he will be forced eventually to become a revisionist of common sense, and introduce subtle distinctions that the latter often "misses" (that is, that it doesn't need at all), for example the distinction between "being" (which applies to all intentional objects) and "existing" (which applies only to some of them); if he takes the second course, he will indeed assert that intentional objects are a manner of speaking, but in a pregnant sense, that is, in the sense that one could, and maybe *should*, do without them—or better, without *a reference to them*—and that if one did so then everything would be clearer.

B: Whereas for you the situation is different?

A: For me, or for the transcendental idealism for which I act here as a spokesman, the statement that intentional objects are only a manner of speaking reduces simply to the following: that we cannot expect them to belong to the ontology, at least not as such, not unconditionally. But ontology is not my starting point: it's rather something to be accounted for in terms of other notions. So what I said is not at all worrisome, and certainly in no way diminishes the use that the *concept* of an intentional object has in explicating the concept of ontology. In other words, for the realist the fact that something is a manner of speaking creates a problem, because for him speaking must in every case find a solid foundation in being; for me, instead, since I begin precisely with speaking and on the basis of speaking look for the sense of the word "being," manners of speaking are my necessary kit of tools, my hammer and nails.

C: A hammer and nails that don't cause too much sweat.

A: Maybe, though the desperation I feel when I try to explain these matters to myself or others seems worse than sweat. Consider also that with one's sweat one builds concrete, physical, solid things, whereas the castles of words I put together give me no such satisfaction: even when I believe I've formulated a thesis in a convincing way, the next time I'll lose it, and using the same words will not guarantee that I understand them.

C: Poor soul, why don't you just forget about it?

A: You're back at the same point, Corrado. I've already answered you, and if you want we can talk it over some more. But now let me finish what I was saying.

B: Yes, let us finish. These intentional objects . . .

C: No, I'm sorry, but I've been patient enough. You refuse to understand—because you don't find it convenient—that the order in which things are discussed is not at all neutral, that treating a certain question *after* certain others has a fundamental influence on *how* the question is treated, and on how important it gets. Some questions have a revolutionary significance just because they're asked when they are, when people are not expecting them, in an "untimely" way. To face them "in due time" would be to domesticate them; to have them preceded by a long "conceptual" development where they "naturally" find their place would amount to defusing their explosive power. There are so many different ways of doing violence, to paraphrase what you said earlier about my verbal attacks, and one of the most subtle is to impose on others the rules of a game they never said they wanted to play, and then to blame them if they don't follow the rules. I don't want to listen to you; I believe that there's something deeply wrong in speaking of these things in this way, and I believe it's my duty—not just my right—to interrupt you and insist that the game, not just the result, can well be different, and that your rules can well be rejected. You, Angelo, who speak so much of revolutions, how do you think revolutions are made, by chatting?

A: No: they're made by preventing others from chatting, without however forgetting to take home one's paycheck.

B: Nice shot, Angelo. Now, while he worries about his responsibilities, let's try to go on. These intentional objects, then, how do you mean to use them?

A: To begin with, to speak of the intentional object of a given experience will be the same as to speak of a property of that experience, that is, to put it in Brentano's terms, of the experience's *intentionality*. A state of anxiety or of depression, or a toothache, are good examples of experiences that do *not* have this property. On the other hand, if I desire or think or see, in general I desire or think or see *something. What* I desire or think or see is the intentional object of my desire or thought or seeing. And once more we must not get confused. The intentional object of an experience is *distinct* from the experience, just as the property *brown* that applies to this table is distinct from the table. Furthermore, the intentional object is not (always) ontologically dependent on the experience whose object it is, in contrast with a property, which is always ontologically dependent on the object whose property it is: no object, no property. For it's entirely possible to desire, or to think of, objects that have nothing to do with us or our mental processes. The only dependence here is conceptual: it's the *concept* of an intentional object that depends on the *concept* of an experience. In other words, to explain *what* an intentional object is one must begin by speaking of an experience.

B: I think I understand. But I'm not yet clear as to how you intend to use this maneuvering room you created.

A: It's because we're only at the first step. As I said, not all intentional objects will exist in my model, so we need to make some distinctions. How? If you return for a moment to the general structure of the operation I'm trying to perform, the next step will appear entirely obvious. I want to provide a coherent way of thinking of our approach to the world without adding anything to the world itself, or deleting anything from it, without making any change within the empirical scope of our actions. Now the empirical world is one of objects, one in which objects are the fundamental preoccupation and resource; hence empirical realism (putting *res* first at the empirical level) is an inevitable consequence of our conservatism. Traditionally, empirical realism was accompanied (awkwardly, as I tried to prove) by an analogous conceptual realism; whereas I want to propose (because of the difficulties one runs into when trying to reconcile the two realisms) an asymmetrical solution, combining empirical realism with some form of conceptual idealism. This means that, while the realist lives in a world of tables and chairs, *and lives in it in such a way that every philosophical justification must ultimately bring us back to tables and chairs,* I live in a world of tables and chairs, where however philosophical justifications, for example of what makes a table or a chair "objective," must be given in terms of ideas, representations, experiences, and so on. There thus arises the following problem: how can I claim with even a minimum of credibility that, beginning as I do in my philosophy from the point exactly opposite to the one from which my life begins and develops—or my experience, if you will, which is not an experience *of experiences* but an experience of objects how can I believe that I will arrive where I want to arrive, that is, at that life, at that experience? For the realist the thing seems automatic, because he starts from the same point on both levels: from objects. Even if his program must face all the difficulties I mentioned, there is at least an initial resonance between the two spheres of his activity, and hence at least an appearance of agreement. But how can *I* substantiate my pretense of empirical conservatism, considering the conceptual revolution I'm preparing? How do I know that I won't be forced to change the world, not just our way of thinking of it?

B: Once more, it seems more easily said than done.

A: Exactly, and, if you'll allow me a digression, it's not by chance that this phrase has occurred more than once in our conversation. Within philosophy we only say things, and often we convince ourselves that what we said is possible only because we didn't say enough. Then we say more and the whole castle crumbles. For example, the expression "empirical realism and transcendental idealism" was all right as long as we didn't ask how to use it: when we did, we realized that we were not at all sure of understanding it.

B: So let's try to understand it better. Is there a way of getting the answers you need within your conceptual system?

A: It would seem so. Suppose you carry out the following two-part operation. *First* you assume instrumentally the realist paradigm, where objects are conceptually primary, and within this paradigm ask yourself what the basic, distinctive features of an object are. *Then* you let go the realist hypothesis but keep the features you discovered, and make them—within the *idealist* paradigm—into conditions on intentional objects (or perhaps on the experiences whose objects they are) that qualify them as real (or qualify those experiences as objective). To the extent that the set of conditions you obtained is complete, you should be able to reconstruct through them exactly the set of objects from which the transcendental realist's reflection starts, that is, exactly the set of objects among which the empirical realist *lives*.

B: Ingenious. Does it work?

A: Not as well as one might hope. In the abstract, the main problem would seem to be finding a complete set of conditions. But in fact one can't even get to that problem, for one gets stuck long before it.

B: What do you mean?

A: That when one carefully considers two of these conditions, one realizes that they contradict each other, and hence nothing can satisfy them both.

B: Nothing? But then . . .

A: Wait a minute, let's go easy here. A fundamental feature of objects as traditionally understood is that they are, *in themselves*, precisely determinable and distinguishable from one another; in other words, we can count them, we can say that this is *one* object and that is an*other* one and together they're *two*. As long as we remain within the realist horizon, this feature doesn't have much bite, for it's entirely legitimate to suppose that there are objects that *we* cannot *in principle* count or identify—not just because of empirical and contingent limitations. That we can't know how many angels can dance on the head of a pin is our problem, for the realist, not the angels'. Things change, however, when one tries to apply this condition within an idealist perspective. For then to say that it's impossible to formulate identification conditions for objects in terms of experiences—that is, in terms that we could, at least in principle, understand and apply—means in the last analysis to reintroduce once more, in addition to experiences or instead of them, conceptually primary objects, and hence to declare failure for our whole laborious project.

B: So these objects must be identifiable by us?

A: Yes, but let's be clear about it: "identifiable" in a purely logical sense. We must be able to think of what it would mean to identify them, taking for granted that quite often the identification will be practically beyond our scope. Unless it were logically possible, however, we might as well forget about the whole thing and admit that the concept of an object is essentially inexplicable, primitive.

B: O.K. And what's the significance of this conclusion?

A: To explain it, I'll give you an example. Suppose you dreamed of a rhinoceros last night, and then you ran into a rhinoceros an hour ago. Question: how many rhinoceroses did you apprehend within the last twenty-four hours?

B: Two.

A: Are you sure?

B: Should I not be?

A: Think about it. "Two" means "exactly two," and "exactly two" amounts to the conjunction of "at least two" and "at most two." Now you certainly didn't apprehend *more* than two rhinoceroses, but isn't it possible that you apprehended *fewer* than two?

B: I don't understand.

A: "At least two" means "at least two *distinct* ones." And how do you know that the two rhinoceroses we're talking about are distinct?

B: Why? Do you mean they're identical?

A: Not quite. I mean that there seems to be no way to decide the question, and in a very strong sense: not because we don't know enough, but because the question is not defined, because there aren't, and apparently one can't think of, identification conditions for objects like this.

B: Whereas there are for other objects.

A: Exactly. Take for example the second rhinoceros, the one you ran into an hour ago, and suppose you run into another one right now. Many things could happen to prevent your deciding whether these two rhinoceroses are identical or distinct: you could die suddenly . . .

B: Let's hope not.

A: All right. So you could fly to Tasmania, join an interplanetary voyage, or simply forget these encounters. It would then be practically impossible for you to solve the problem of the identity of the two animals, but this doesn't mean that you don't know how in theory one should go about solving it.

B: Of course: one should reconstruct the history of the third rhinoceros, through documents and witnesses . . .

A: And possibly—a very important matter—by tracing some causal chains backwards, to prove that at a certain time it *had to* be in a certain position . . .

B: That's right. All this until one arrives at the point where I ran into the second rhinoceros.

A: Very well. So you can describe the conditions under which the two rhinoceroses would be judged identical, and at a conceptual, philosophical level this is all that matters. Whether one can actually apply such conditions is an empirical problem, which doesn't influence our capacity to *think* of the verification procedures—indeed in a sense, to say it *à la* Kant, the actual verification *is made possible* as a meaningful, well-defined problem precisely by this capacity.

B: A transcendental argument, then?

A: You can call it that if you wish. I don't like the expression "transcendental argument" very much, because it's often been used to mean an almost magical attempt to refute the skeptic by complicated logical virtuosities, which would supposedly end up proving him conceptually confused. Whereas I think that there's no confusion at all in Hume, that indeed he puts in a brilliant light the traditional realist's confusion, and the program I'm presenting is not *against* Hume, but if anything *starts from* Hume: it's a program that accepts his destructive conclusions and makes an effort to articulate *another* conceptual model. Within this program, and hence in substantial agreement with the skeptic, one can find (or believe one finds) logical necessities like the ones we've just discussed, and if one wishes, since the argument develops at a conceptual, transcendental level, one can even call it a transcendental argument, as long as it's clear that it's not a philosophical argument of some special kind. Like all philosophical arguments, neither more nor less than the ontological one or the third man, it's located within a definite theoretical context and purports to establish, for those who accept the hypotheses holding in that context, some consequences of such hypotheses.

B: All right. But, if I'm not mistaken, you started out with the intention of showing the problems that arise within the idealist context.

A: Yes, but the path that will take us to the problems is long and tortuous. The first conclusion we reached is the following: It's practically a tautology to say that objects of experience are in time, since time is the dimension of our consciousness, *distentio animi*. But to be able to identify and count these objects—which we judged essential in order to pass a positive judgment on their existence—something more is needed than a temporal location. What is needed is a *spatio*temporal location; indeed, more precisely, we need to locate them (in principle, of course, not that in fact you or I, or the whole of mankind, must be able to do so) within a unitary (spatiotemporal) system of causal sequences.

B: I don't see any problems yet. Indeed, these sound like important results.

A: And they are. But now let's turn to another fundamental feature of objects as traditionally understood—one that we could call *substantiality*. It's this: an object is considered categorially distinct from properties and relations. One thinks of it as something that can and must be the ontological support of properties and relations but must not be reducible to them—otherwise, it would lose its objectual character.

B: The object as a substrate, you mean?

A: Exactly, and you know very well that, with all its difficulties, this notion exercised a constant attraction on classical metaphysics, which always despised any attempt to see objects as pure and simple aggregates of properties and relations. If objects are the conceptual starting point, it's with them that one must begin when writing the world's catalogue, and if it's this realist notion of an object that we're trying to reconstruct within the idealist scheme, then even substantiality must find a place in our reconstruction.

B: But the attempts you mention are typical outcomes of empirical idealism, which as you (and Kant) said derives in turn from transcendental realism. Within your new framework we should be better equipped conceptually to avoid conclusions like Hume's (and Russell's) that a rose is an aggregate of a certain color, a certain smell, and so on. After all, it seems that you proposed your revolution just to escape conclusions of this kind.

A: You're right, and in fact *these* conclusions can be avoided. But unfortunately analogous ones are looming.

B: The plot thickens.

A: True. One can't deny an element of authentic surprise in this chain of reasoning, as always when absurd conclusions follow from entirely natural premises. But let's go one step at a time. We said that an intentional object can't be regarded as existent if it doesn't have a spatial location.

So let's take this table, which undeniably has such a location, and inquire about its substantiality.

B: There seems to be no problem. Certainly the table is distinct from its properties: its being brown, smooth, rectangular . . .

A: Yes, but it's not from this direction that difficulties arise. We must ask whether the table may not itself *be a property*.

B: What do you mean?

A: The table is in space, and space is divisible. So let's consider the result of one such division, say into molecules, that is: the set of all the molecules constituting the table. Question: are these molecules objects?

B: I don't see why not.

A: Me neither. But the molecules could get detached from the table, individually (and then we wouldn't notice it) or collectively, generating a (small) catastrophe that would bring the table to destruction and the molecules to follow different destinies. This is to say that there will be a table, this table, only as long as a certain set of molecules, in some sense continuous with the ones present now, maintain a certain set of properties and mutual relationships.

B: I don't understand what you're driving at.

A: I'm already there. Nothing keeps us from regarding the table as an object and attributing properties to it, but the troubling thing, emphasized by our reasoning, is that nothing keeps us from seeing the table *in another way, too*, that is, as a complicated system of properties and relations among a certain set of molecules. The space occupied by the table is identical with the space occupied by these molecules (at a given instant), so dropping the table wouldn't create any gap. It's certainly boring, and it may be impossible, to follow all the molecules in their wanderings, and speaking of a macroscopic object like the table is a useful way of summarizing their behavior. But this doesn't rule it out that in principle one could do without this device, or rather avoid reifying its pragmatic value, and limit oneself to saying that the table (even better: a name of the table) can work as the subject of a proposition—as indeed virtually anything can, including obvious properties like being brown or rectangular.

B: Now I understand. What you say is true and seems confirmed by the following observation. The domain of chemistry is the entire spatiotemporal universe, without residue; however, the ontology of chemistry includes no tables but rather molecules. Which doesn't mean that tables cannot enter it, but if they do it's only (implicitly) as those very complicated systems of properties and relations among molecules you're talking about. So the possibility you're considering is not a purely theoretical one: it's a real choice among different ontological alternatives, and undeniably in one of them there are no tables as objects but only molecules.

A: Your example is a good one but I wouldn't insist on it, for it might suggest that our conclusion depends on the actual assumption of a given ontology within scientific research. And this is not the case. Our only premises, if you remember, were that the table is in space and that space is divisible. That one in fact divides it may be useful to bring out the point, but it's ultimately irrelevant. Even if science, for its own reasons, had established that there is an ultimate ontological level to which all others must be reduced, to the extent that objects at that level are still in space—and for us they *must* be, to count as objects—it's always logically possible to divide them.

B: Certainly molecules can be 'divided, too.

A: Indeed. All I said earlier about the table can be said for each of the molecules constituting it, and for each of the atoms constituting those molecules, and for each of the subatomic particles constituting those atoms—and in fact all of this was said, step by step, within atomic and then subatomic physics. But the most important thing for us is that, even if it had never been said, even if no one had ever found it useful to say it, its conceptual validity wouldn't be diminished by an inch, and I repeat: its validity not just for molecules, atoms, protons, quarks, and all other entities postulated by science so far (or in the future), but also for all possible parts of those entities.

B: So it's enough to be able to divide something in thought?

A: It's enough for us, at least to throw us into despair. For consider the conclusions we reached. First, objects must be in space to be identifiable. Second, nothing in space can have that character of ultimate substantiality which seems an essential feature of an object.

B: But then there can be no objects.

A: Nothing can work as an object in an absolute way. More precisely, we can't expect any intentional object to satisfy once and for all the reality conditions we decided to gather by our realist "mental experiment." Only one avenue is left, which however will turn out to be largely delusive.

B: What would that be?

A: Remember that you yourself were speaking a little earlier of alternative ontological choices. This word "choice" is quite suggestive, for it's precisely by a choice, a *decision*, that the chemist or the physicist or, if you will, the carpenter privileges a certain level of analysis of reality, and disregards all others. The physicist knows that he *could* well assume an ontology of tables, and the carpenter knows (if he's sophisticated enough) that he *could* well assume an ontology of particles, and it's not out of the question that at some other time they might indeed assume them, but at *this* time, dealing with *these* specific problems, other ontologies are simply put aside, without scruples or regrets, just as one decides without too much thought, almost automatically, that to drive a nail he needs a hammer, and hence it's better to put aside the guitar he's got in his hands.

B: Once more, then, you suggest an instrumental view of philosophical results.

A: More precisely, I suggest that the outcome of philosophical reflection is an instrumental view of the world. But we may return later to this aspect of the situation; now I would like to draw your attention to something else. A choice is always made for some purposes, and these purposes define a *context*, within which what is impossible in an absolute sense becomes often quite natural. Let me explain. If my present purpose were, say, to have dinner, my ontological choice concerning the portion of spacetime immediately before me would certainly lean toward a table, whereas if my purpose were to find an optimal solution for waterproofing this surface, it's likely that the idea of "positing" a table wouldn't even cross my mind, and I would turn with no hesitation to an ontology of molecules. In other words, when one leaves the global level typical of philosophical reflection and takes into account concrete situations, there seem to be no great difficulties in determining the most appropriate ontology.

B: But then the problem is solved.

A: Really?

B: Yes: it's enough to clarify once and for all that the criteria of objectivity gathered through your expedition into the realist universe are to be applied locally. These criteria, that is, will not let us establish that a particular intentional object is real, or is an object *tout court*, unconditionally, but only that it is real in a specific context, in connection with specific purposes. Where this assertion of locality, remarkably, can be made in an absolutely universal way—indeed it represents an additional interesting *general* result of your research, on a par with the one obtained earlier concerning spatiality as a necessary condition of existence. What do you think of this?

A: It sounds very promising, and in fact I, too, once believed that it would work. But it doesn't, unfortunately; this is one more case in which things seem to add up only as long as we stay on the surface. When we go deeper, the illusion of having reached some definite result dissolves without a trace.

B: I'm really curious to know where the mistake is.

A: It's not exactly a mistake. What you said I could subscribe to, with no afterthoughts. So there is a rational inquiry that establishes necessary (and, one hopes, collectively sufficient) conditions for making objects of experience move legimately from logic to ontology. Such conditions are, as one would assume on the basis of their rational character, entirely universal; among them, we have for example identifiability, substantiality, then others we haven't discussed like, say, some sort of coherence, and finally we have the one you called locality. This last one says that the other conditions must be applied at a certain level of analysis, determined each time by the context of application and the purposes present and active in that context.

B: Perfect. I couldn't have put it any better.

A: I put it so well because, as I mentioned, I thought about it for a long time, and at some point this hypothesis was not just tempting, but had me completely convinced.

B: And then what happened?

A: I asked myself a simple question. I said: "Suppose I've now concluded my rational inquiry. It's not at all clear that such a conclusion is possible, that one can ever be assured of having reached it, but suppose for the sake of argument that we have. So now I know that, in every context where I find myself, an object of experience will be considered real only if, *for the purposes relevant to that context*, it counts as identifiable, coherent, and so on. Let's consider the next context I happen to be in, and ask ourselves what the use of this knowledge is."

B: What do you mean, "what the use is"?

A: Bertoldo, you're the one who says that the project of rational reconstruction of the world expressed by philosophy is not an end in itself or, at least, it's usually not been conceived that way. It's not just that the philosopher has fun understanding how things are; indeed, he would be the first one to think that he understands nothing unless he could convince himself and others that his understanding makes a difference, that it makes it possible for him and the rest of mankind to live better, to prosper, to be happier and more successful. Remember Aristotle's *Metaphysics*: intellectuals are wiser than manual workers because they understand the principles of the latter's activity, and can possibly guide it toward a more effective outcome. And remember the Cartesian tree: metaphysics is the roots, physics is the trunk, and the branches are the various applied sciences, so the world can now be better *primarily* because philosophers understood it.

B: Yes, I remember, and I agree. Why, do you think that the knowledge we're talking about is good for nothing?

A: "Everything," "nothing," "something" are generic terms, often interchangeable. Let's rather try to establish with a minimum of precision *what* this knowledge is good for. So, I'm placed in a specific context, I'm considering a specific intentional object, and tell myself: this object is real to the extent that, for the purposes relevant to this context, it's identifiable, substantial . . .

B: O.K., O.K., and then?

A: Don't you realize the vacuity of the expression "for the purposes relevant to this context"? How far does this context extend? What are its boundaries? The last five minutes? The last twenty-four hours? The last five minutes in my life, the lives of the people around me, of mankind? And when I talk about the purposes relevant to this context, am I referring to the explicit ones, those which crossed somebody's mind and might even have been put in words or written down? If this is what I'm referring to, very few purposes are at work in any context. Or am I referring to the purposes that can be reconstructed from the behavior of the people acting in this context? But then the number of purposes expands so much as to challenge any possibility of control.

B: Just a moment. You're going too fast and asking too many rhetorical questions. Now more than ever we need to proceed carefully, or at least I do.

A: You're right: I got carried away. I mean that we're in the presence of a gigantic vicious circle. Our original problem arose from the indeterminacy of the spatiotemporal continuum, within which it wasn't possible to isolate any object without making a definite choice. This choice, however, we said must not be understood as an arbitrary move: it's rather a "natural" consequence of certain purposes. What purposes? Those holding in the context where the choice is made. And thus the problem seems solved. But it's not: we didn't solve it, because the word "context" is just as indeterminate as the spatiotemporal continuum we started out with. More explicitly, any action can be located in an indefinite number of contexts, of different (spatiotemporal) width, where different choices turn out to be natural. If the context of my present behavior is limited to myself and the last five minutes, an ontology of tables may be the most natural one, whereas if it's to be understood as mankind facing the world during this century, it may be just as natural to put it in terms of particles. So, instead of solving the problem, a reference to the context seals its mystery, for in order to use the expression "the context" meaningfully one must postulate the very act of choice among infinitely many alternatives that that reference meant to account for.

B: Quite a depressing outcome.

A: You said it; still it would be simplistic to conclude that our inquiry was useless. It did achieve something: not what we thought, or wanted, it to achieve, but certainly not nothing.

B: I feel better already. Jokes aside, I can't see the use of a theory that has no practical applications.

A: And you won't see it as long as you understand the relation between theory and practice in terms of the scheme mentioned earlier: a theory gives a more or less accurate image of the world, and on that basis proposes practices that work because (and to the extent that) the theory is accurate.

B: How can we see this relation in any other way?

A: Suppose you did something strange, something that doesn't at all fit your habits, for example you gambled a lot of money and lost. You yourself can't understand how it happened, and wonder for a while whether you lived through an episode of true insanity. Which worries you: such episodes, if they occur, can occur suddenly, without any apparent reason, whatever our (superficial) state of physical or mental health. What if another one occurred, when you least needed it? What if next time you didn't just lose money? You keep ruminating on what happened, and suddenly you're hit by a connection: just that morning you had done something that couldn't be considered a crime but troubled you nonetheless. Who knows?—you had taken advantage of your office in a way you despise, though it's socially quite common. So you tell yourself: "Sure. What I did later is perfectly logical: it's neither insane nor meaningless. Since I felt a need for punishment but my behavior was not legally punishable, I punished myself." With these words you've certainly given an explanation for your behavior, but one that tells you nothing about the future. Even if you believe it, you're not entitled to any conclusion concerning the next time you'll feel guilty; you know all too well that whether you then punish yourself or not, and the way in which you might punish yourself, will depend on factors that are now totally unpredictable. In other words, your explanation, your "theorization" of what happened, has no practical application.

B: Which is why, I would say, it's no explanation.

A: Sure, that's what you would say if you were doing philosophy in an "official" way. Damn it, one must defend one's scientific respectability! But now we're only having a conversation among friends and you can relax. Specifically, you can admit for a moment—just to follow the thread of what I'm saying—that the sort of behavior I described is fairly common, that people ordinarily consider it *explaining what happened*, and that maybe, though your philosophy of science tells you that this is no explanation, it should probably limit itself to saying that it's an explanation that *differs* from some others, for example the ones given in physics, but still has its dignity and (why not?) its function.

B: I'm beginning to think Corrado is right, and that one shouldn't even let you start talking.

A: Maybe, but now you've let me talk a great deal and are too curious to know how the story ends. I promise I'll be brief. The psychoanalytic explanation you gave for your behavior has no predictive value. Does it mean that it has *no* value? Consider your state after you gave this explanation. Beforehand you were nervous, dissatisfied, you felt as though you couldn't trust yourself any more; now you understand, everything makes sense, you brought your life back into order and can happily return to your everyday activities. Shall we say that your mental state changed because the explanation was the *true* or *right* one? In a way this question has no answer, not because we don't know the answer but because the question is wrong, because it has wrong presuppositions and goes in the wrong direction. The explanation you gave is right *because* you accepted it, made it yours, and by means of it returned your life to order and coherence. There is no preestablished reality to which this explanation must be adequate in order to be true; *you* make it true when you appropriate it and make it fulfil its function, which is to tell your experience as a story with a beginning and an end. So my proposal is simply this: to consider the philosophical explanation of an event as an operation of the same kind as the one just described. Both are directed not to the future but to the *past*, they're attempts not at determining what will happen but rather at fitting what has already happened into a coherent system. Both have the primary purpose of quieting down our anxiety, of convincing us that what happened didn't happen by chance, that the world makes sense. Both have only one criterion of validity: they're good if they're accepted, *because* they're accepted, and if they're not accepted then all external authorities or objective facts are irrelevant. And finally both, just because there's nothing external they must face or come to terms with, are burdened by the implacable destiny of always appearing somewhat arbitrary, like a magic spell that convinces and reassures us more through its sound and rhythm than through what it says.

B: But *do* these "explanations" say anything?

A: Frankly, it depends on what you mean by "saying." Let's return to our table, and suppose we've chosen, at a given time in our story, an ontology including it. Afterwards, we try to rationalize our decision, we invoke the operational context and the purposes relevant to that context, and we point out the local significance our rational criteria of objectivity derive from that context and those purposes. We say that the table is (or was) a legitimate member of our ontology because it's identifiable, substantial, etc., where the words "identifiable," "substantial," etc. are understood in the sense appropriate to the context in question. All this is quite satisfactory, it makes us feel that the situation is under control, that we did the right thing, yet still we can't help noticing that, had we chosen a different ontology, we could have justified it by using the same words ("identifiable," "substantial," etc.), and hence the same "rational criteria," and simply changing the "context" in some suitable way. There's always a context fit to justify our ontological choice, whatever it may be, and this insinuates the suspicion that our exalted rational criteria are just empty words that "say" nothing.

B: By your reasoning, this seems much more than a suspicion.

A: True, but why? Because the myths imposed by traditional realism condition us totally, and convince us that the only "significant" way language can work, the only way we can use it to "say" anything, is by building declarative statements that communicate *facts.* It's only when we say things like "The sun is shining" or "The earth is rotating" that we actually say *something.* But this is not true. We needed Wittgenstein to notice how seldom language is used to state facts, and how often it's used for other purposes—to reassure and comfort each other, for instance, or to condition us or do us violence. Well, within a model of the workings of language that allows for greater flexibility and doesn't want to force us to speak like the news—or better, as a naive ideology imagines the news speaking—within such a more plastic and discriminating model one could admit that philosophical explanations of the kind I described "say" something.

B: All this is ingenious, and sounds sensible. Too sensible, maybe. If I remember correctly, you said earlier that your philosophical explanations were burdened by the destiny of appearing arbitrary. Why burdened? What destiny? From what I hear now, it sounds as if this destiny is nothing but a contingent consequence of adopting a questionable model of the workings of language, and probably of thought, too. Let's get rid of the model, and we'll get rid of the evil destiny.

A: Unfortunately, it's not so easy. The questionable model you're talking about is not just any model: it's the realist one. And we can't get rid of this model without complications. If you consider again the way I phrased my program, you'll remember that it didn't just consist in formulating a transcendental idealist alternative to classical metaphysics but also, and most important, in a delicate operation of translating the demands and criteria of that metaphysics into the new paradigm. Only the hypothetical completion of this translation seemed able to ensure that agreement with empirical realism which in turn constituted an irreplaceable condition for our empirically conservative attitude. To abandon transcendental realism for good would mean to lose any conceptual contact with our ordinary, everyday realism, and hence once more to declare the failure of our project of conceptualizing the world—if only because there would be nothing left to conceptualize. Consequently, in spite of all the limits that I critically recognize for the realist model of language or of anything else, I can't help keeping it as a constant term of reference, and feeling strongly the dissatisfaction it causes for the more or less ingenious solutions I'm able to find.

B: Then what?

A: Then I see no alternative to accepting the conflictual situation that has come about, and digesting the fact that the final agreement theorized by the original program is impossible. If we had been able to complete the translation I suggested, if the realist conditions of objectivity had turned out to be interpretable without residue within the system of transcendental idealism, then the contrast between the two paradigms would have resolved itself into a temporary event. *Before* the completion of the program, that is, there would have been a contrast; *afterwards* it would have been clear that the realist theses, *once adequately interpreted*, were wholly acceptable, and one would have achieved—the idealist would have, at least—that universal comprehension which Corrado (sarcastically) attributed to me. But, since the program *cannot* be completed, this comprehension is unreachable and the realist paradigm remains a foreign body, a continual source of infection.

B: Go easy with the metaphors. This last one is a bit obscure.

A: Biologically speaking, an infection is a struggle. Bacteria and antibodies face each other, and the resulting yellowish pus is a brimming river of their corpses. As long as the struggle is on, the organism must be on its toes, with eyes well open, and the alteration in the body temperature is a consequence—and a signal—of this state of alarm. Watch out for any relaxation, any letting go, any lowering of defenses! That is the greatest danger: the quiet that would follow is the quiet of defeat.

B: Very eloquent. But what does it tell us?

A: It gives us an analogy to the state in which one finds oneself when trying to combine transcendental idealism with empirical realism. Since there is no "final solution" available that definitively harmonizes the two positions, one must maintain both, in an always precarious and unstable equilibrium which can't resolve itself in either direction without neglecting some fundamental needs. One must let oneself be guided by realist schemes within everyday life and at the same time (or better, at a different time, that is, when one has turned to philosophical reflection) *critically* remind oneself that those schemes are fallacious, that the image they project, if examined from a transcendental point of view, must be judged an illusion—one that is probably inevitable for those who want to preserve ordinary beliefs and practices, but still an illusion.

B: Wait a minute, don't go too fast. Tell me again why the realist is under an illusion.

A: Not an illusion *tout court*, mind you: a *transcendental* illusion. That is, an illusion at the conceptual level: the illusion of one who, while refusing certain schemes of interpretation of the world and not being able to translate them—and hence to some extent justify them—within the schemes he accepts, is still constantly forced to use them, and hence must keep repeating, almost obsessively: "I behave as if these schemes were valid, but know in my heart that they're not."

B: The conclusion is quite dramatic, indeed I'd say melodramatic. But are we forced to accept it? Can't we rather turn it around, as in a *reductio* argument? You started out with the difficulties raised by Hume and other skeptics for a realist conception of the world. But those difficulties didn't constitute a true refutation of the realist program: they only brought out the fact that the program had not yet been successfully completed. In your reading, Hume challenges the realist, telling him in essence: "You may not realize it, but you haven't yet given me a coherent way of thinking about the world, about my experience and knowledge of it, and possibly about many other things as well." And I can even admit that Hume—or better, *your* Hume—is right. In the face of this challenge, however, what is your reaction? To declare defeat right away and abandon transcendental realism. Isn't this decision too rash? Wouldn't it be possible, instead, to accept the skeptic's challenge within the realist scheme and do one's best to find a solution there? How do you know that it's the scheme's fault and not the fault of those who've used it so far? But let's even put aside these considerations, for the moment. Despite everything, your proposal is somewhat reasonable. You say: "So far, an impressive series of powerful minds have tried with blind determination to solve this problem by using these tools, to no avail. Maybe it's the tools that are inadequate. Let's bring in other tools and see if we get a better result." All this, I repeat, is reasonable, and sounds like things we read, for example, at the beginning of Descartes' *Discourse on Method*. So we follow you patiently and scrupulously in your journey to see where you're going, and you, after a whirlwind of assumptions and arguments and a few vain promises to be brief, where do you get? To a position in which, if we want to keep our ordinary realism, we must do it almost by generous concession, as a gift to a poor idiot who otherwise wouldn't be able to move. To a conception of the relations between theory and practice on which theories have no other use but to soothe our anxiety, and which not only admits psychoanalytic explanation—this sort of scarecrow in the philosophy of science—without justification but even assumes it as the model of what an explanation should be, at least in philosophy. To a vision of language in which the latter "says" something not by stating facts, telling us how the world is, and letting us transmit information, but rather by reassuring us and quieting us down, by patting us on the back and making us feel less lonely. At this point, with all the good will in the world, I feel forced to respond that your revolution promises no good, and that as far as I'm concerned I prefer to remain faithful to classical metaphysical schemes. If I can't make them work, I can always think that it's my fault, which—I assure you—leaves me feeling a lot better than the conceptual catastrophes you propose, and the state of permanent civil war that seems to be the outcome of your program.

A: How can I blame you, Bertoldo? With your robust common sense you have brought out clearly the circular structure of my argument. You will remember that at the beginning we mentioned the possibility that conceptual inquiries might have empirically significant results. You defended this possibility and I denied it. But *I didn't argue* for my denial. All I said was: "We'll discuss it later." Now *is* later, and you may have understood my reasons: the conclusion—if we can call it that—of my conceptual inquiry points to a total lack of relation between philosophical reflection and empirical practices. The latter work, though they proceed, indeed possibly *just because* they proceed, in a direction that reflection considers delusive and fallacious, while reflection desperately tries to fill the gap of our misunderstanding with a set of words about which we have no idea whether they mean anything and which in any case have no practical value—not directly at least. If they're good for something, they're not good for what they (apparently) *say* they're good for: they're good more *because they are said* than for their alleged content. You understand all this, and understand that it was to be expected, that in fact the result was already written in my initial methodological choice. If I had believed that language can reach the world, and dissolve into a transparent interpreter of factual reality, I wouldn't have let myself be seduced by the verbal pandemonium that I put together and that left me—predictably—empty-handed. Convinced that what matters is what one says, not how one says it, and hence that the choice between languages, or between paradigms, is ultimately irrelevant, I would have continued with perseverance and determination to look for things, instead of blaming the locutions handed down to me and looking for ingenious new ways of expressing my ignorance. I got what I deserved: I put on blue glasses and ended up seeing everything blue. A sensible person's reaction before this gigantic "useless machine" is entirely obvious: "To hell with paradigms and translations, to hell with intentional objects. Let's return to serious work with the usual tools, and we'll get something: not everything at once as this madman wanted but *something* nonetheless, which is more than he got. We've wasted too much time listening to him."

B: You won't tell me that you spent all this energy just to conclude that I'm right?

A: No, I won't tell you that, but only because I don't want to, not because I think you're wrong.

B: Here we go again. You said you would avoid useless paradoxical statements. Explain yourself more clearly or you'll prove me right once more, since this last statement, taken literally, merely confirms my original suspicion that your subtle reasonings reduce to a gratuitous and childish play—if not a dishonest one. And you'll prove Corrado right, too, more right indeed than he himself thought when he called you a fraud. For he called you an *unconscious* fraud.

A: O.K., I'll try to be clearer. To begin with, from the fact that I don't think you're wrong it doesn't follow that I think you're right, admitting for the sake of argument, as we seem to be doing implicitly, that you take the transcendental realist's side. As I see it, there can't be right or wrong in such cases, for without premises nothing can be argued, without arguments nothing can be proved, and without proofs nothing can be justified. But, since the choice we're talking about, between a realist and an idealist conception of the world, is probably the most general one in philosophy, it's natural to think that it works as a *premise* in a philosophical system, and that there's nothing *more* general from which to derive it. Therefore I'm (trivially) right on the basis of my hypotheses and you're (just as trivially) right on the basis of yours—or, more correctly, neither of us can accuse the other of being wrong. Your earlier harangue had the great merit of showing clearly that my initial reference to (true or alleged) difficulties in the realist scheme was at best a rhetorical artifice, which didn't establish the incorrectness of that scheme. However, while I'm perfectly willing to accept your harangue *now*, I wouldn't underestimate the importance of using that rhetorical artifice *then*. If it's true that the two positions are *theoretically* on a par, it's also true that one was for a long time more popular than the other, and because it was more popular it was also elaborated with greater attention and diligence than the alternative. If the alternative is to reach true equality *at the practical level*, it must be developed, articulated, explored in its manifold potentialities, and for this purpose even a bit of propaganda like the one I smuggled in at the beginning can have its function.

B: In a minute you'll say that you must lie to me for my own good.

A: I'm not exactly sure what a lie is; one day maybe we should talk about it. But I know that it's often possible, saying things that are technically true but saying them with a certain tone, in a certain order and using certain words, to *make* people do more or less what one wants. Now it's technically true that transcendental realism faces certain difficulties, but citing these difficulties at the beginning and those of the idealist alternative only at the end was certainly important to making you listen for so long. This is however—I repeat—a common practice, and I wonder whether I'm morally worse than my neighbor only because I'm more aware of using it.

B: You're right: this topic would take us too far. So go ahead with your "theoretical" self-defense and leave a discussion of your moral qualities for another day.

A: All right. From my point of view, then, there is nothing questionable in the fact that a point of view—at least one of the level of generality at which we're moving—can only be justified from the inside, that is, in the last analysis, in a circular way. It follows that there's nothing strange, for me, if my methodology to some extent already presupposes my conclusions. But, you will say, *once I arrive at these conclusions*, why should I persist? What kind of image do I have of myself at work, as I pursue with so much determination, one might even say so much obtuseness, a philosophical program from which, by my own admission, I will get no wisdom, that will not make me function better or reach my goals more effectively? In the same rhetorical, propagandistic terms I used, what hope do I have of selling this merchandise to anyone, what hope do I have of selling it to myself? If it's reassurance that I think I need, isn't it much more reassuring to go back to speaking about things? Things, at least, remain firm and stable, and if problems arise they're our own, they can in principle be solved, and in any case they don't threaten the structure of the ontological framework.

B: I couldn't have said it better. And now I'm anxiously waiting for an answer.

A: The answer I'll give you is not new. Once more it's a thesis I mentioned at the beginning, and then "skilfully" dropped. Remember when you said that philosophy sounded like science-fiction, and I told you that the comparison was on target but for the moment we could leave it at that? Well, now a comparison is no longer enough: the time has come to be more explicit.

B: If I'm not mistaken, you were talking about philosophy as some kind of play, which like all play is useful to prepare us for still unrealized possibilities.

A: The accuracy of your memory would be amazing if I didn't know that thinking as clearly and lucidly as you do is the best recipe for maintaining a firm control of one's experiences. But let's get to the point, and let me begin by articulating this metaphor of play a bit. First step: the child. If you think about it, there's little the child *has to* do. All he needs, others will do for him. His function is almost exclusively a consumer's: of food, of time and energy, and even of knowledge. So if we adopted a traditional, Aristotelian model of the relation between theory and practice, there would be no reason for the child to do anything else, and no explanation for the fact that he indeed *does* something else. He's not strong or resistant enough to carry out useful tasks, and hence—according to this model—should limit himself to accumulating, on the one hand, energetic resources that make him grow and, on the other, data that at the right time, when he's acquired an adequate physical structure, he might put to profitable use. But, strangely, the child spends most of his time—or, maybe better, *would like to* spend most of his time—doing useless things: handling swords and kitchens and brooms and tractors, indeed (most often) *pretended* swords and kitchens and brooms and tractors. How can we account for all this? Shall we say that instinct, that infallible guide in selecting the behavior most advantageous for the individual's and the species' survival, misfired just this once? What could be the sense, the purpose, of this vain activity?

B: That of training for future tasks.

A: Sure, and in this connection consider the following two things. First, the biological necessity of such training (which we must admit if we don't want to think of ourselves as evolutionary dead ends) proves that education can't be reduced to the appropriation of data, to be used when the situation requires it. There is something deeply wrong in the traditional idea that practical application is an inessential, though possibly useful, appendix to theoretical knowledge: learning also means moving, repeating certain routines until they get boring; and hence so much the better if they never do, if this tireless repetition (which, mind you, bores the adult) is part of a playful game.

B: All this is reasonable, but it's no big news. It's commonly believed, for example, that one can recite a physical theory by heart without necessarily being able to do the exercises. And in a way one really knows the theory precisely when one learns, by practice, to apply it to dripping faucets or celestial conjunctions.

A: O.K., there is a sense in which we all know these things. Scientists know them as well as elementary schoolteachers, computer programmers, tailors, and shoemakers. But somehow when we do philosophy of science, and maybe even of education, we forget them, and talk about objective tests and theoretical tools of prediction and control, as if they were the only things that matter.

C: Everybody tries to sell what he's got.

B: Look who's back. Did you come out of your existential crisis, Corrado?

C: You guys go ahead. I was speaking to myself.

B: At least you're speaking aloud again: I thought we had lost you for good. Returning to our theme, Angelo, this last distinction of yours sounds like a special case of your revolutionary "politics." There is nothing wrong in the educational practice *per se*, but one must revise its philosophy.

A: Though it sounds peculiar to hear you apply to my position the general/particular scheme I'm criticizing, I believe that in your language this may be a fairly accurate reconstruction of my story. With one qualification, which I already made but which it won't hurt to repeat. If I don't call in question the ordinary, say educational, practice, it's not because I regard it as correct. Quite often I have absolutely no idea about its correctness, since I'm not familiar enough with the issue, but even when

I do have an opinion I don't have it as a philosopher, but rather as a scientist or a tailor or a shoemaker or an educator, and as such I'll take all the relevant risks and responsibilities, without waiting for philosophy to guide me with its words of wisdom.

B: Objection sustained. And now let's move on to the second thing that I believe you wanted to consider.

A: O.K. An interesting aspect of child's play is the following: even though, *while they're playing*, children abandon themselves to their activity with total dedication, such enthusiasm usually doesn't turn into monogamous faithfulness. Children, that is, like to play different games at different times—many different games. Variety fascinates them, novelty conquers them. Mastering one game is not enough reason to give up others; indeed, a game that is fully mastered may well become boring. Now all this could have a simple justification: if play is training, then when a particular kind of training has fulfilled its function it's a good idea to switch to another. But this justification may be too simple. For, if we look at things once more in biological-adaptive terms, it's natural to ask ourselves: wouldn't it be better if there were a limit to this process? When he grows up, the child will only do a limited number of things; why then should he train for so many others? Isn't it a waste of time and energy?

B: One could answer that the child doesn't yet know, biologically speaking, what he will do.

A: And it would be the right answer, so long as the emphasis is placed not so much on the individual as on the community. For an individual, it might indeed be more advantageous to concentrate obsessively on a single activity.

B: In fact it looks like it is. Think of tennis or chess champions.

A: Right. One could almost say that these child prodigies—I would call them *idiots savants*—turn to their individual ends the community's biologically determined altruism, just like someone who throws his garbage in the street in a generally well-behaved country and gets the double advantage of sharing in generally clean streets while making no effort. These are the true evolutionary dead ends.

B: I believe I understand what you're saying, but I want to make sure that I'm absolutely clear about it. So don't skip too many steps and tell me in detail what this biologically determined altruism consists of.

A: It consists of the following: it's an advantage for a community if the greatest possible number of its members train, and are thus prepared, for the greatest possible number of activities—even activities, we should note, that don't yet have and possibly will never have any practical value.

For the environment where the community lives presents a great variety of problems, and besides it evolves, and problems evolve and develop with it. Any activity can be seen as the solution of a problem: the more solutions are available, the better the community will be able to survive and prosper. Keep also in mind—and here we go back to the first consideration—that one must get ready well ahead of time: when a new, maybe even serious, problem has already come up, it may be too late. Knowing its causes, having an extremely sophisticated theory about it, being able to predict its evolution will not help: we will need someone who's already able to move his hands in the right way, and hence who's already moved his hands that way when the problem was not yet a problem, *only in play*.

B: O.K., but this training must come to an end at some point.

A: In general, it ends with the end of adolescence. And it's not by chance that the latter is being extended: the world gets more complicated every day and hence requires an ever wider spectrum of operational capacities, to be acquired through the apprenticeship we're talking about. At any rate, for most people the apprenticeship does come to an end: one stops playing and begins to act for real. Which means: one selects a specific activity from the many one has learned, and begins to get bored with it in a way that is immediately profitable—not just long term or from a communitarian standpoint. But, like all rules, this one too has its exceptions. There are moments when the old playing habit gets center stage again, and there are even adults who make a profession of this habit.

B: You mean professional players?

A: No, they don't play at all; I mean those who think the least about play. But let's take it slowly. I said that the child was the first step in articulating our metaphor. So let's move on to the second one: thought.

B: You won't tell me now that thinking is playing.

A: That's precisely what I will tell you, but in due time. Before that, we must treat of mice for a while.

B: Mice? You really like to show off your originality.

A: No, that's not it. In fact, what I'm going to tell you now is the least original thing I have to say; Konrad Lorenz said it already, more or less in the same terms.

B: A bit of stealing, eh?

A: Let's give it a more dignified sound and call it contaminating—in the Latin sense, I mean. So you put a mouse in a new environment, say one of the usual mazes, but a maze where the mouse has never been, and what does it do? It runs through it frantically, gets into all the aisles, opens all the doors, bumps against all the walls, and not just once: repeatedly.

Finally it stops, and one would like to ask: Why all this? Was the mouse perhaps looking for food? No, it had just eaten. Was it then trying to calm its anxiety, the fear generated by that foreign environment? Maybe, but still this answer says nothing: it doesn't explain why one should fear a foreign environment, why a secretion of adrenaline and a consequent raising level of attention and activity should be the most natural response in such cases—and hence, we must assume, the most adaptive.

B: Because a foreign environment can hide dangers.

A: Not even that says much. For what is a danger? Something troublesome or perverse that we must deal with? But there are a whole lot of troublesome and perverse things in whose face we're able to go to sleep! And so much the better that we are, for otherwise in some situations—say, in war—we would no longer sleep—and would end up losing the war.

B: Maybe the decisive element is that in a foreign environment there are unknown dangers.

A: Right, and at this point we may well drop the word "danger." Objectively, a tightrope walker is in great danger, but this doesn't make his heart go much faster. But suppose now that the same man is unexpectedly summoned to court, where perhaps he's never been, and try to imagine him in the waiting room. Don't you see him nervously pacing back and forth, in total analogy with the mouse's frantic movements?

B: I believe you're right. But why should fear be an adaptive reaction to the unknown?

A: Not fear so much—that is, the phenomenological counterpart of this process. Fear is, as Freud would say, nothing but a signal—the more effective the more acute and unpleasant it is. It's rather the behavioral consequences of fear that matter: specifically, the fact that the mouse, by getting excited in this way, moves, inspects the threatening environment, and thus step by step exhausts its resources and potentialities, appropriates it. After pushing all the levers, running down all the aisles, and opening all the doors many times, the mouse is ready: now it can properly respond to that environment.

B: That is, it knows it.

A: "To know" is a phrase that can be easily misunderstood. I won't object to your using it, as long as it's clear that it adds nothing to what I just said: knowing the environment, at least in this case, means adequately responding to it.

B: A true behaviorist attitude.

A: I can accept that label, but always with the qualification "transcendental." The empirical thesis that (within the scope of psychological studies) there is nothing but behavior has no interest for me, indeed (as a psychologist) I would strongly criticize it; my thesis here is the *philosophical* one that the *concept* of behavior must be the starting point in our semantic explanation of the psychological universe of discourse.

B: Sooner or later we must call in question this distinction between empirical and transcendental. You seem to use it too often—and somewhat uncritically—to get out of trouble.

A: You're absolutely right: we will question it. But for the moment let's leave the mouse aside and consider one of us, a human being in an analogous situation of stress—say, in a cell. It's certainly possible that the man, too, will behave like the mouse: we said earlier that it wouldn't be strange if he were literally to take steps in the new environment. Under stress, there is a certain tendency to regression—and one that is probably adaptive, too. When the stress is moderate, however, it's also possible that the man will behave differently, that is, that instead of moving physically, spatially, back and forth in the cell, he will move indirectly, as it were, that is, will let his thoughts move.

B: Go slow with your metaphors. How can thoughts move, if they're not in space?

A: I couldn't explain it in detail, but fundamentally it's a substitution process: instead of moving things, one moves words or images associated with them—where this "movement" consists of going from one word or image to another, of building stories with them, of telling oneself more or less explicitly *what would happen if* one were to take so many steps in that direction, or swing one's arms, or go on one's tiptoes.

B: Counterfactual stories, in sum.

A: Exactly, in a literal sense. For the alternative would be doing those things, making them factual; but talking or thinking about them instead of doing them is much more economical, it requires a much smaller investment of energy. At any rate, aside from this (important) practical aspect, note the resemblance to child's play. In his cell, the man has, we may assume, no specific problem to face, but prepares for all the problems the new environment might create for him by practicing "in a disinterested way," by getting to "know," if you will, the space and the objects around him.

B: So here we are at thought as a form of play. Then the people you mentioned earlier, who make play into a profession, should be thinkers, philosophers.

A: That's right, though this formulation might generate a misunderstanding to which we must return later. For the moment, I believe I gave a reasonably clear explanation of what I mean when I assert—or rather, when I agree with your assertion—that philosophy is science-fiction. Whereas ordinary people indulge in these playful activities only in exceptional circumstances, say in the presence of a "danger," or in marginal ones, during occasional regressions to childish behavior (holiday rites, alcoholic catharses, menopausal crises), but in general are well advised to follow with rigorous and automatic efficiency their codified instructions, it's advantageous for the community to have a number of people available who practice childishness as a job, or a vocation, and may even get paid for thus playing with words and generating imaginary problems and equally imaginary solutions. Many of these problems will remain forever imaginary, much as many of the tasks a child performs while playing will never be part of his life as an adult, but it's enough if *some* become real for this activity to be an extremely useful component of the social fabric. So much more useful, I will add, the less it crystallizes, the more possibilities it explores, the crazier the stories it tells. A philosophy that sits still on results already acquired, that repeats the "safe" lessons of the past, is not just boring: it's harmful, because it runs exactly contrary to its task.

B: No schools, then, in philosophy?

A: You've got it right, and you're also pointing to an inevitable tension in this profession—which is responsible for the misunderstanding I mentioned earlier. I said that the presence of philosophers is advantageous for the community, but this doesn't mean—as one often thinks—that it's advantageous for it to have official institutions where philosophers can work. For such institutions tend to remain constantly identical with themselves and to encourage conformism in their members, that is, the most counterproductive attitude a philosopher—as such—could have. It follows that, when we talk about the room the community must find for philosophy, it's best to understand this room as changeable and informal, and the people occupying it as unlikely outsiders who enjoy kicking the ball around, almost at random, not as members of an academic corporation tyrannically devoted to enforcing "objective" and immutable criteria.

B: But isn't this an exaggeration? Didn't you say that one needs time to articulate stories, that it's useful to create "free areas of intervention and exchange" in which to discuss and "see what the situation is"? Why couldn't academic institutions be precisely areas of this kind, why couldn't they give you all the time you need for articulation and research?

A: Because an institution must be something definite, with a set of rules, with well-defined "institutional" tasks, established once and for all. It's just as well that things be so, for all the functions that it makes sense to institutionalize: government, justice, the banking system. But here we're talking about a practice that contradicts all definitions, denies all boundaries, mocks all prohibitions. We're talking about a way of "articulating" ideas that might frighten the very people who had the ideas in the first place. So the time to conduct this operation must inevitably be found in private, away from any institutional context.

B: Indeed, it's a commonplace that philosophy is never done at the philosophy department.

A: And like all commonplaces it makes sense. Which doesn't mean that the people doing philosophy shouldn't work and be paid in a department; in my opinion, however, they do philosophy precisely to the extent that they remain at the margins of the tasks for which they are paid, or even oppose them. At any rate we're finally able, after this long digression, to answer your original question. Articulating a new philosophy is a value in itself, and if in order to convince people to do so it's necessary to use the rhetorical artifice of referring to the difficulties of the old philosophy then let there be artifice, let there be rhetoric, let those lies come forth that will earn us heaven.

B: It's undeniable that all you say—while you say it—sounds fairly convincing. In your own terms, you not only have a theory about the importance of rhetoric, but also seem quite good at practicing it. Still, when I put together things you've said at different times I feel some tensions, almost contradictions . . .

A: I don't doubt it, since certain things can only be said at certain times, at certain points in the story.

B: Maybe, but this is not a monologue, or if you will it's not only your story. It's also mine, and at this point in my story there is this much to say: that you've given two rather dissonant characterizations of philosophy. On the one hand you depicted it as an activity with its own scope, separate and distinct from the scope of other activities; you spoke of a "purely conceptual" practice that must neither disturb nor be disturbed by empirical practices, of a semantical analysis that must reveal the meaning of those (other) practices without interfering with their development. Now, however, this alleged chasm between philosophy and the human species' other kinds of behavior seems to dissolve: not only is philosophical activity justified on the same evolutionary and adaptive basis that you (apparently) apply to all other activities, but its structure is far from unique or extraordinary. Doing philosophy is like playing house or pirates, only for longer and more pervasively. What shall we do then with your initial "transcendental" pretense? Where shall we locate the universe of concepts that was

philosophy's habitat, its neglect of empirical reality, in this perpetual
carnival we ended up with?

A: Well said. And all the more because, I repeat, this is—for me,
at least—the time to say it. I have insisted often that one can't say
everything at once, and that one has the right, indeed sometimes the
duty, to say things in the order most advantageous for them. At this
point, my story has gone far enough, it is sufficiently mature and used
to walking on its own legs, to be able to face your challenge with good
hopes of survival, whereas a couple of hours ago the same challenge
would have killed it, at least in your eyes. For it is a challenge: to jump
into the void with no net, without the comfortable alibi of old words
repeated like magic spells. You're now asking me to question those
words, and *now* I can do it, now indeed I *want* to do it: I want to
clarify once and for all, to you and to myself, what's hidden behind
the mystery of philosophical transcendence.

B: I'm all ears.

A: You yourself said—in agreement with Kant and many others—that
the level of rational reflection at which philosophy moves results from a
process of *abstraction*. But "abstraction" means "separation," so the problem arises of understanding what things are separated through this process, and how. Traditionally one thought that everything had a form or
essence perceptible by reason and expressed by concepts, and a spatiotemporal matter that situated it in the ephemeral sublunar world and made
it accessible to the senses. According to this model, then, one thought
that abstraction separated form from matter and gave us the most authentic and durable identity of the thing itself, what the thing truly was;
whence all talk of an immutable world of ideas, of the eternal truths that
inhabit it, and so on. Within the revolutionary perspective I propose, on
the other hand—a perspective that, it might help to point out once more,
I certainly don't believe I discovered there is only one world: that of our
practical operations, of our moving hands and mouths, and of all the
things, physical things I mean, that make us move our hands and mouths
or possibly prevent our doing so. Is there still room in this world for a
process of abstraction, of separation? Separation of what, and from what?
The answers to these questions have already been given; it's just a matter
of retrieving them. I've already said that thought has primarily a counterfactual significance: instead of doing something and suffering the consequences of it, we *think* of what could happen if we did it *but we don't do
it*. Now how, *in concreto*, does this counterfactual reasoning work? It works
by stretching and adapting consolidated practices. The adaptation may

be minimal, as when it comes to walking around in an unknown room: the room is indeed unknown, but we certainly know how to walk, we have done it so many times, in so many different situations, that we don't need too much imagination to know what it would mean to walk *here*. And sometimes the adaptation may be drastic, as when we try to imagine what would happen if suddenly a computer started asking us questions about our political opinions, and possibly criticizing them. But, drastic or not, the adaptation always works in the same way: by taking certain modes of behavior, acquired within a certain field of activity, and applying them (or rather, applying words ordinarily associated with them and hence such that they can "represent" them) to a somewhat different field. That is, by separating them, "abstracting" them from their usual associations. It's this kind of abstraction that governs play, at least play conceived as invention and fun, rather than as a repetitive ceremony; it's the same kind of abstraction that governs thought, understood as armchair exploration of unrealized possibilities. And, finally, it's this kind of abstraction that is at work in philosophy, playing with words and images, combining them in unpredictable, surprising ways, constructing systems that are—that must be—nothing but castles in the air.

B: So, concepts . . .

A: . . . are words left to themselves, drawn out of the contexts where they're applied safely and automatically and made to wander in the void of a not yet well-defined alternative application, in the total uncertainty of what is or is not proper to this application, in the frantic search for a new sort of assurance which, however, once achieved, will have already carried us *outside* philosophy, outside this essentially metaphorical or, maybe better, metonymical activity, this continuous exploration of novelty which refuses in principle to settle down, which defies by vocation all rules.

B: Your fear of not being understood makes a lot of sense. It's as if at every step you reinterpreted all the previous ones, continuously reshuffling the deck, or at least the meanings of all the cards.

A: Well said. And this procedure fits my idea of philosophy as a progressive dislocation of practices, as a ceaseless decontextualization of some components of those practices—a possible premise to the generation of different practices. At this very moment, I'm doing philosophy, that is, I'm forcing received kinds of behavior in new directions. At the beginning what I say sounds familiar, it uses established locutions, old tools of the trade like "conceptual level of analysis" or "necessary conditions of objectivity." The hearer is reassured by this vocabulary and believes he has sufficient control of the situation to be able to explore the new "contents" I'm trying to express without falling at once into an abyss of incomprehension and absurdity. But then, step by step, those locutions are violated, tried out within new scopes, used in more and more deviant ways. One has the impression of the rug being constantly pulled from under one's feet; still, if the operation is performed delicately, it's possible to stand the resulting vertigo, and even enjoy it as one sometimes does with a very strong feeling.

B: I must admit that there is a certain (maybe perverse) coherence in what you say, and that its very self-applicability is fascinating, but if you don't mind, in spite of all your delicacy, I keep running into the same problem, that is, your thesis that philosophical research is factually irrelevant. Initially I thought I understood your position; I didn't share it, but at least it sounded reasonable. One carries out some sort of abstract inquiry, and on the basis of it concludes that there is an unbridgeable gap between transcendental criteria and their empirical application, and hence that the criteria will never be informative concerning that application. It's a perfectly decent conclusion, which one might disapprove of without judging it absurd; the way I see it, it's the old Humean problem of induction more fashionably phrased. Now, however, after this reinterpretation of conceptual activity itself, I feel lost. If abstraction is understood in the traditional way, as a separation of a thing's form from its matter, one can claim with some credibility that the results of this abstraction have no implications—or at least no direct implications—for the universe of concrete practices. After all, the world of ideas is *another* world, and it's plausible that something essential might get lost in moving from the one to the other, that by eliminating matter we might also eliminate all possibility of a concrete approach to everyday things. But, if abstraction is understood as you just said, this kind of justification goes by the board. How can you, while constantly emphasizing the stepwise character of the estrangement that philosophical activity consists of, claim that there is a total lack of communication between this activity and the others? Why shouldn't the science-fictional play that is philosophy tell us something about the world, at least about some marginal aspect of the world?

A: I could give you a very simple answer, namely that if we drop the assumption that we can discover a form of things, we also lose any guarantee that separating such things from their concrete contexts will serve any purpose. Playing is certainly fun, I could tell you, and perhaps even useful, but there's no way of knowing in advance in what specific way it will be useful. Consistently with our earlier conclusions concerning the *a posteri-*

ori character of our reflection and of the resulting explanations, it's only the adult who can say, when he finds himself in possession of a skill he's acquired by playing as a child, and is aware that this skill is useful: "Ah, that's what playing was good for." But I don't want to give the impression that I'm undervaluing your question, nor do I want to deny that there's something deep in your continuing to express the same embarrassment in different ways. For I've certainly used old philosophical ghosts somewhat tendentiously in order to introduce my view. I've spoken, as you correctly remember, of transcendental conditions that are not satisfied at the empirical level while suggesting, or at least without explicitly denying, that all this would be, in turn, the final destination of a conceptual journey, hence of a *forced* journey, analytically necessary. But now the chickens come home to roost, and the issue is to know why I didn't just say, "*I cannot know* whether philosophical play is of any help," but wanted rather to say, "Philosophical play *cannot* be of any help."

B: I feel I should expect a further distortion of the sense of words.

A: Right. Once again, we're going to add a new dimension to our discourse and, once again, this dimension must be added now, *after* all the work we did, or we would have risked getting stuck at the very beginning.

B: Let's prepare then to see another example of creeping revolution take place.

A: Your political allusion is perfectly appropriate, because it's precisely about politics that I want to talk or, better, about the moral evaluation contained, more or less explicitly, in every political action. In short, the necessity I refer to when I claim that philosophical reflection can't have direct empirical results is deontic, not alethic, and as such applies primarily to *the philosopher*, that is, to the devotee of this strange practice of renewal, and only secondarily to his discipline, to *what* the philosopher says and does.

B: It's we, then, who cannot and should not have any empirical effect?

A: Exactly, it's you and I and Corrado and all the others: we're talking about us. And we're doing so, once again, in terms of the general problem of the relation between theory and praxis, and of what follows from my rejection of an Aristotelian conception of this relation. Let's try to summarize. I deny that the philosopher is the sage who reaches a (more or less) correct vision of the world and is able, on the basis of this vision, to direct the rest of mankind and provide his fellows with a more effective approach to the environment. My view is that the philosopher is an eternal child, a pathetic kid who in old age still finds delight in senseless riddles and absurd little tales. Far from having anything to teach, he tends to be laughed at and, as old Thales did, to fall into wells from looking at the sky too much: he's a fool, a clown, whose statements often sound like irresistible puns. Question: is it convenient for society to let a fool of this sort do what he does, and even praise him and give him awards? Answer: yes, in order to survive the inevitable turns of fortune (read: the sudden transformations of the ecosystem) a society must be able to afford a certain number of philosophers, who investigate and question with maniacal determination the most obvious things—precisely the things that most people would (rightly) find it ridiculous to investigate and question, but that could suddenly be exploded by the turns of fortune, leaving us to deal with a situation out of our control. The philosopher will perform this task so much better the more foolish his hypotheses and the more peculiar his statements are, the more he's ready to call even himself in question, and not let himself be put to sleep by the soothing repetition of familiar phrases. And it's just as well for society to grant him a respect his stories don't deserve, and an academic position and a delusive reputation for wisdom: no one likes to look silly, so probably no one would find this activity attractive unless there were some dividend, some halo to crown the *rex sacrificulus* who takes it up. But beware of exaggerating, of taking the thing too seriously! What the philosopher does can be compared to an experiment in a laboratory, where in artificial conditions a certain number of variables—that is, components of a real situation— are isolated (I would almost say "abstracted") and then played with, usually in a disinterested way, which sometimes happens to have remarkable practical consequences. And the philosopher's is a very dangerous experiment, no less risky than those in a laboratory of nuclear physics or genetic engineering; as in those other cases, then, one needs great caution not to end up facing a virus or a reactor gone wild. Playing with the received foundations of our most common practices is playing with fire, even if the play occurs vicariously, that is, through language, for its most natural tendency is to expand beyond language, beyond thought, all the way to *things*.

B: Would this be the reason why the philosopher is always seen as a pain in the ass?

A: Exactly. The philosopher himself, with a few brilliant exceptions, is inclined to see this conception of him as the result of a general bad faith on the part of the community, and one that it's necessary—though painful—to shake off in the name of the True and the Just. But as a matter of fact the bad faith is his own, it's he himself who doesn't realize the significance of his activity. The others—they already have the True and the Just, since they already have established habits on which to base such value judgments. Whereas he not only does not yet have these habits but as a philosopher will never have them, and so in a way is a pain in the ass just for its own sake.

B: Which doesn't rule out, if I understand you correctly, that his work has a function.

A: No, to be sure, just as the fact that many make love for its own sake doesn't rule out that making love has a function. In the philosopher's case, however—and who knows? maybe in the lover's, too—it's to a large extent an unconscious function, indeed often one he would *deny* if it were suggested to him—whence the bad faith. A bad faith that, as I've already indicated, is probably essential to this strange individual's continuing his activity without his falling into the deepest despair, as indeed maintaining a certain distrust toward him and his stories is essential to the community.

B: A distrust that occasionally goes all the way to the hemlock or the stake.

A: Yes, but in such cases one must not demonize the community, or conversely deify the philosopher. What happens is a disgrace, and it would be better if it didn't happen, but still it's only the malfunctioning of a mechanism that ordinarily fulfils a very important task, and that it would be foolish to try to eliminate merely because *sometimes* it creates problems.

B: What mechanism are you talking about?

A: We already discussed it a little while ago: it's the fear, the horror even, that arises spontaneously when we're faced by an even minimal distortion of the rituals that constitute our successful adaptation to the world. I'll give you an example. Once, as a stunt, it occurred to me to switch the positions of my feet as I was driving, putting the right on the brake and the left on the gas.

B: A very stupid stunt.

A: If you will, but also in a way a philosophical one. Well, the feeling I had was one of authentic, uncontrollable panic, and if I hadn't immediately returned to the usual position I would certainly have crashed. Why the panic? Because my life depends on mastery of this particular prac-tice—driving, that is—and so it's of the utmost importance that every-thing in it be done correctly, with no imperfection, safely and automati-cally. To any variation from this automatism, the most effective response is a good negative signal, such as the horror I experienced.

B: A horror that saved your life.

A: Yes, and this is the kind of horror that ordinary people often feel toward the philosophers' "inconsiderate" proposals, their continuous insistence that everything should be called in question, their challenges to the most elementary convictions, those most indispensable for the working of society. This horror, too, saves lives, the community's and its members', and in this case, too, it's not necessary that the horror claim any victims. When it does, when philosophers are burned or poisoned, it's because the mechanism jammed; most often, it's enough to isolate the lab where philosophical experiments are carried out from the houses, the factories, and the offices where ordinary existence continues—and where the premises questioned by philosophers must continue to hold, *until one has proof of their falsity.*

B: So what you're saying is the exact opposite of the slogan "Power to the imagination."

A: That's right. As I see it, the normal behavior of the social organism (to use my biological metaphor once more) depends in this case on a certain balance between two factors: the freedom manifested in philosophical play and the resistance opposed to it by the powers that be—not least among them public opinion. When this balance is present, the system is able to incorporate useful new elements without losing the compactness necessary for its survival. When the balance fails, the system runs into more or less serious trouble—of two different kinds, depending on the two possible kinds of instability. On the one hand, the pressure exercised by the institutions may become too strong and repress, even violently, any diversity however small; on the other, free play can spread too far and infect the whole community. Bonfires of books and humans are a manifestation of the first kind of trouble, the ravings of Jacobins and terrorists of the second.

B: So you're saying that the revolution must be frozen?

A: Yes, frozen in a lab, and its results must be introduced into the community gradually, cautiously, and only when it's absolutely necessary. Which finally justifies, to return to our original problem, isolating the conceptual level of philosophical research from the factual one of everyday life: an isolation that, as I suggested earlier, perhaps a bit obscurely, is a question not so much of what is as of what ought to be the case. And justifies the fact that the philosopher is limited—must be limited—to counterfactual reasonings, to stories locked in a universe of words, that is, of substitutes of things, with all the (insoluble) problems thereby generated for establishing the reliability, the significance of his results.

Letting him play directly with things would certainly provide a better guarantee that he's not running around in circles, but it would be too risky.

B: It sounds like everything fits in your position, and I think I see how you would respond to some obvious objections one could raise.

A: Such as?

B: Such as: if you were told that your empirical realism has now become a sort of consecration of existing institutions and practices, and that the "useful new elements" you mention are nothing but a verbal trick to make you look better, since your model doesn't allow for the (however minimal) revolutionary import they would undoubtedly have—if you in sum were accused of being a fascist, a tired epigone of the miseries and atrocities of Hegel's ethical state—it would be easy for you to answer, insisting on your biological metaphor, that it's all a matter of degree, of how much revolution a community can tolerate in a given period without dying out.

A: Right, and also that, perhaps, it would be best to save the word "revolution" for changes exceeding this threshold.

B: And if you were accused of refusing *a priori* to give a sense to history, and of reducing it to a blind entanglement of environmental transformations and adaptations to them, you would probably say that in your system there is also a place for the attempts to discover a goal and a rational direction for our various vicissitudes: that these attempts are an essential part of the same play of adaptation, because without the "transcendental illusion" manifested in them, without the carrot of understanding how things work, the stick of the changeable external demands would not always be sufficient to move us.

A: That's right again. With an important qualification: the stories that make sense of things are often used by both parties, and thus contribute to the balance I was talking about. There are revolutionary stories proclaiming that, given the way the world is, certain changes are necessary, and there are conservative stories explaining instead that the situation and community where we live are the best possible ones and hence it's absurd to look for alternatives. The latter stories, too, have a function, insofar as they offset the former, and here, too, philosophers can be very useful; in this case even "institutional" philosophers, the wrinkled mummies operating (so to speak) in academia. For the revolutionary thinkers' creativity may leave entirely speechless those who are not used to this kind of play, so it's appropriate to have, on the side (and in defense) of the inexperienced, some other players endowed with, if not the same creativity, at least the same skill and experience.

B: Yes, I understand. Still something doesn't add up.

A: What is it?

B: Your role in all this.

A: But it's obvious: I'm one of the many clowns telling these stories, individually useless but (maybe) globally advantageous—though, in any case, advantageous for reasons that I, for one, could only consider wrong.

B: I knew you were going to answer this way, and your answer is consistent with all you've said so far. But, paradoxically, it's an entirely theoretical consistency: there seem to be no contradictions among your statements. At a practical level, however, at that behavioral level which in your view is the only one that really matters, something is amiss.

A: What do you mean?

B: It's difficult to say it clearly, and besides I didn't spend my time, as you did, turning *your* position inside out. My own gives me enough to worry about. But something puzzled me repeatedly as you were talking, and sounded as if out of tune: you were always too content and satisfied with what you were saying.

A: Why shouldn't I be?

B: Yes, why? I can't give you a direct answer, but if you don't mind I'll try to think aloud, and perhaps with your help my thoughts will take a more precise form.

A: I am at your disposal.

B: Good. Then, to begin with, you know that there are pragmatic paradoxes, that is, sentences that describe perfectly possible situations but nonetheless could never be used by anyone to make true statements.

A: Sure: sentences like "I'm not here" or "I do not exist."

B: Precisely. The person who says, "I'm not here," might well not have been there, there's no necessity in his being there; still, given the way we use the word "I," that is, to indicate the speaker, and the way we use the word "here," that is, to indicate the place where the speaker is, it's impossible for a speaker to say anything less than absurd by uttering the sentence, "I'm not here."

A: No objection so far.

B: So let's take another step. There are pragmatic paradoxes that arise in cognitive contexts: sentences like "It's raining, but I believe it isn't," or "I know that it's raining, but I might be wrong about it." Here, too, the two members of each conjunction could well be true together but, given the way we use the words "believe" and "know," no speaker could reasonably utter such conjunctions.

A: I'm with you.

B: Then take the sentence, "I know nothing." Once more, the situation described by this sentence is not impossible: it's not impossible, that is, that the speaker knows nothing. Is it possible, however, for a speaker to say something true by uttering this sentence?

A: Go on.

B: I don't think so. Because, if he says something true, he says something he knows, and hence knows something.

A: Wait a second: saying something true is not sufficient for saying something one knows. At least one must also *believe* what one says. I could arbitrarily combine words of a language I don't speak, and end up uttering true statements, but this wouldn't mean that I *know* what I'm talking about.

B: Do you mean to tell me that when you state your theory, and claim that philosophers have no wisdom, that they play with words, that if they say anything useful they say it for the wrong reasons, you don't believe these things?

A: That's right: this, too, is a story, one of the many.

B: But then why do you tell it?

A: Because it's always better to have one more story.

B: Who says that?

A: The story.

B: And do you believe it?

A: No.

B: Now I'm sure not following.

A: That's because you keep reasoning in the old way, on the basis of an abstract wisdom that guides our concrete operations. You keep thinking that *because* one believes something, one does something else, whereas I insist that one acts first and believes later, that is, tells a story about what one has done—which includes the story I just told, and what I'm saying right now. But we have already seen how ubiquitous the realist conditioning of our language is, so the only way to fight it, to defeat the tyranny of these declarative sentences, which allegedly state *facts*, is to say them and then deny them, construct them and then destroy them, exactly as I'm doing here.

B: O.K. You have an answer for everything. But perhaps I took the wrong route. Once more, as I watch you and listen to you, I feel that it's not *what* you say that bothers me, but *how* you say it, and that the problem should be put not in cognitive but, I would say, in emotional terms.

A: You did say earlier that I shouldn't be so happy.

B: Right, and with my reference to pragmatic paradoxes I was trying to articulate this feeling. But in the process I lost it.

A: Try again.

B: O.K., I'll try one last time. Maybe we should extend the concept of a pragmatic paradox to capture what I have in mind. Can a person say "I'm desperate" while displaying the nicest smile in the world and continuing to have great fun? Wouldn't you think that one who behaves like that does it for some ulterior motive—who knows? perhaps to seduce a pretty girl by playing on her maternal instinct—and hence that his behavior is insincere and unfair, false not in a cognitive but in a moral sense?

A: Yes, I would probably find something wrong and questionable in it.

B: Well, it's in this sense that your attitude doesn't ring true to me. Socially, your profession—*our* profession, I mean—is considered the depository of a great deal of the available wisdom, and you yourself say that this reputation, however misplaced, is useful, maybe even essential, to its success. When the philosopher speaks, it's almost inevitable for all others to feel a sense of inferiority, to feel they are not up to par. People may laugh, as they did with Thales, but they laugh to overcome their embarrassment, and in any case the philosopher is ready to use that laughter for his own purposes, to strengthen his mysterious authority with petulant and provocative statements; think of Heidegger, who, referring just to Thales' episode, defines philosophy as what makes housemaids laugh. Now you in some sense dispute all this, and claim that the philosopher is foolish, but while you dispute it your style remains the usual one: sharp, ingenious, subtle, and above all self-assured. You behave exactly as philosophers have always behaved, generating (I think) the same intellectual respect they've always generated, but denying at the same time that they're due such respect. And it's here that you seem dishonest to me. I'm not saying that you should change jobs, because in your own way you're convinced—sorry, "your story says"—that philosophers can still be of some indirect use, but at least I would expect to see you a little more troubled, more distressed, more saddened by your incapacity to reach wisdom. And you're not: you remain the usual philosopher, preachy and irritating, ambitious and verbose. If at least you could think, as many other philosophers have thought, that what you say is true, there would be a subjective justification for your behavior. But no, you say it doesn't even make sense to speak of a true story, yet still the thing doesn't seem to bother you at all. Once more, I can't help thinking that you're making improper use—morally improper, I mean—of the intellectual gifts you undeniably possess.

A: Would I be morally more praiseworthy if I beat my chest and shed warm tears while saying exactly the same things?

B: Not if your chest-beating were a fake, but yes, if it represented a true existential conflict, an awareness—intellectual *and* emotional—of the contradictory, paradoxical nature of your activity.

A: And prevented my effectively carrying out this activity.

B: Maybe, if carrying it out effectively involves this fragmentation of one's personality, this mediocre opportunism which recites the *mea culpa* in the tunes of the *gloria mihi*.

A: You're always the same: always trying to reach theoretical consistency—in this case, of the individual.

B: But you, too, said that consistency is a criterion of objectivity, and hence something that we should at least search for.

A: Sometimes, and sometimes not.

B: I can't make myself clear.

C: Bertoldo, you're pathetic.

B: Thanks a lot. What a nice remark, after such a long silence!

C: No, look, don't get mad. I didn't intend to blame or criticize you, but in some sense to praise you.

B: Praise me?

C: Yes, praise you, for your moral uprightness, for your honesty, which prevent your understanding Angelo's message but make you a better man.

B: Better and duller, you seem to be saying.

C: Yes, maybe duller, too, but only because you keep playing the same game, by the same rules, and *this* game you play probably better than any of us, better even than Angelo, who was forced by your diligence to express himself with unusual clarity, and not think that he could get off the hook with lofty words and fancy digressions. His superiority to you—if we can call it that—is due to the fact that he, on the other hand, doesn't always play the same game, and thus fools you. Incidentally, that's how he plays poker, too.

B: Really?

C: Yes: the others try to concentrate, to reason, to work out the odds, to remember cards, while he shouts, tells jokes, pretends to be drunk, and ends up confusing everyone.

B: Unfair at that game, too, then?

C: Probably, if we assume—as we should, this being a form of social behavior—the point of view of the others. They believe they're playing poker, and the rules of poker include no such moves. But if, for a moment, we leave aside all moral considerations—on which as I said I'm entirely in agreement with you—and limit ourselves to asking what the others should do in order to win against him, the answer is quite natural: they should realize that, willingly or not (indeed, willingly, since they're too nice to make him shut up) they're in fact playing an*other* game, one that possibly *includes* the rules of poker but is not (only) poker.

B: They're playing at who speaks the loudest, or can best pretend to be drunk.

C: More accurately, they're playing at who, speaking loudly and pretending to be drunk, can maintain enough lucidity to coldly evaluate his cards. And at this game Angelo is virtually unbeatable, if for no other reason than that he's the only one to play it systematically.

B: You think that the situation is analogous in philosophy?

C: Exactly: in this case, too, his game is wider than yours, and what makes it wider is that not all his rules are explicitly formulated. But, in contrast with poker, his game here can have a value that goes beyond personal advantage.

B: Try to be clearer. What rules are you talking about?

C: The game usually played among philosophers, as you rightly noted, consists in looking for the truth, finding it, and then presenting it with great arrogance and presumption. Now Angelo wants to put forward the thesis that philosophers find no truth and are nothing but clowns. Suppose then that he acted like a clown, or he became troubled as you suggest: the other philosophers would immediately disqualify him and declare that he in fact *is* a clown or a psychopath, and hence that his opinions—whatever they are—have nothing to do with their profession and don't even deserve to be refuted. But Angelo doesn't act like a clown, *he acts like a philosopher* and, with the same arrogance and presumption as the other philosophers, pronounces his own ignorance. Within the limited scope of his personality, this behavior reduces to a small-time ruse, analogous to the one displayed at the poker table, which lets him live comfortably and attain a certain amount of notoriety by profiting from the ambiguity. Socially, however, the thing has a useful effect, because it doesn't just *say* but *shows in concreto*, with an example in flesh and blood, the falsity and duplicity of these alleged role models—the same duplicity I manifest by maintaining the social status of an intellectual, and taking home a salary for a job I consider useless.

A: You should be satisfied, Bertoldo! There you have the duplicity together with a sense of guilt!

C: Yes, and the inefficient duplicity.

A: Which, on the other hand, finds ample moral justification in its suffering.

C: You're probably right about that, too.

B: But then you agree with him!

C: I agree that there must be people like him, perhaps, and like me. And at the same time I envy his capacity to live in this situation without apparent tension, without pain. Or maybe I loathe it, as one loathes something foreign and incomprehensible, the alien object of science-fiction movies. Or should I say "philosophy movies"? At any rate, I believe that, if there must be someone doing this job, it's better that it be like him. I should go till the fields.

B: But don't you think you're going too far? Sure, if you accept his conclusion that philosophy is nothing but an empty stirring of meaningless words, then it's certainly better to have a philosopher like him, whose emptiness is written all over his face. But this conclusion is not necessary. It's the insistence on the separation between abstract reflection and concrete work that entails such depressing consequences; why then should we not reject the separation, and see philosophy—much like science, though at a higher level of generality—as a way of ordering and systematizing our approach to the world, our *empirical* approach, I mean? What's wrong with the *old* conception of the relation between theory and practice, after all? At bottom, Angelo told us that he disputes it to see what happens, which may well be reasonable from *his* point of view but is certainly not from *mine*. Before throwing overboard a tool that has such a long history . . .

A: . . . of delusions and failures . . .

B: O.K., but why should the mistakes of the past limit the future? All disciplines made mistakes before getting on the right track, so is it strange if *this* discipline, the most abstract and general of all, takes longer to get there? What we need is not your "rhetorical" utilization of old and worm-eaten enigmas, but a rigorous determination of the significant theoretical problems and a definite commitment to face them with solid scientific methodologies.

C: What can I tell you, Bertoldo? I envy you, too. You, too, have your certainties, genuine this time, and you, too, will do your job well. I am caught in the middle.

B: But why do you let yourself be caught in the middle? Why don't you adopt a more constructive attitude? You won't tell me that Angelo has convinced you?

C: Not in the details, primarily because I didn't pay too much attention to him, but it's undeniable that, when it comes to personal taste, to my inclinations, I feel myself on his side, or rather on the side of what he *says*, which makes it impossible for me to *do* what he does. It may be because of how much exploitation, how much pain, and how much blood I've seen emerge from behind the pretenses of wisdom of the "technicians" of printed paper and wordplay, because of how many lies I've seen proclaimed in the name of truth, and because of how many petty profits those lies have earned—it may be because of all this that I can't take any of it seriously. Which means, unfortunately, that I can't take *myself* seriously. The irritation I voiced earlier against Angelo was irritation against myself, as I realized the moment he attacked me: instead of stirring me up, of infusing me with new aggressiveness, his somewhat childish nagging found open doors and solid alliances in me. Meanwhile, he kept talking, talking, and I became more and more convinced that his vicious and complacent ingenuity was the best way to defeat the lies and the violence that frightened me, and for which I felt and feel partly responsible. A king that presents himself naked and in a clownish attitude can always get out of trouble by saying that he was joking, but a king naked and deadly serious is stuck. So, while I'm not that interested in the specific subtleties of his argument, I'm interested in its outcome, which is the well-known outcome of old: discourse bites its tail, and *says* that it does, so let's forget about it and do the *things* that matter, for example care for one another. And I'm interested that it is somebody like him who says this, and that while saying it he never for a moment abandons his royal pose as king of words and discourses, thus letting everyone *see*, not just *hear*, how things are.

B: But why do you want to give up a tool that could make the world better, that to some extent has already made it better?

C: This claim could be questioned, but now I'm tired. Indeed, not just now: I'm tired in general. I hope I'm wrong—for you and your enthusiasm.

B: But in this way you end up accepting all he says. Don't you see him grinning triumphantly as he hears you virtually repeat his conclusions?

C: Don't worry, Bertoldo. However much he smiles and feels pleased, he, too, has his cross to bear. He might leave others speechless, might surprise them by continuously changing tunes and rules, might even build a self-satisfied middle-class existence for himself this way, but he will never be able to say, to himself or others, what his grin would like to express: "See, I was right."

Clarissa

BERTOLDO: Where're you always going with your books, Clarissa? Why don't you sit by us, here in the shade, and have a glass of this sparkling wine—just the thing to bring out deep reflections and smart comments?

CLARISSA: I wouldn't mind, Bertoldo. But I'm in trouble. I have a report due for tomorrow's seminar and still have a pile of stuff to read.

B: What do you mean, "in trouble"? The night is young. A little chatting with friends and a small dose of alcohol will stimulate new and revolutionary ideas, which the world will receive with admiration and wonder.

C: Bertoldo, you're beginning to sound exactly like your mentor. Maybe because you know that you'll get his position. But I think you're right: a little rest will do me good. I've been obsessed with this research for months.

ANGELO: What a splendid example of violence and abuse!

B: What are you talking about, Angelo?

A: You mean you don't see it? Clarissa is trying to get rid of centuries, of millennia of female exploitation—an exploitation based not least on a misunderstood "intellectual" superiority gained by brutally limiting the "other half of heaven's" free time and frustrating all its enthusiasm in an orgy of everyday gloom and pseudoromantic banalities. She's desperately trying to emancipate herself in her own eyes and those of others, to project an image of herself and her role with which other women might identify and from which they might draw courage. And all this is difficult, of course, because of the conditioning she must overcome, and perhaps because the task she's proposing to herself doesn't immediately resonate with her intuitions. But the dominating male feels threatened, worries that these beautiful, precious subjects might rebel against their stupid, ferocious yoke, and immediately intervenes to reestablish the traditional equilibrium. His moves are as obvious as they're effective. Sarcasm first: "Where are your going, poor soul, where do you think you're going? Would your work feel so burdensome, if it came naturally to you?" Thus the circle is closed and the system legitimized: the effort liberation costs is itself a manifest sign of inferiority, so it's evidence that *one has no right* to liberation. Then, after insinuating doubt, interrupting the concentration, mortifying the opponent's morale, here comes the flattery, the soothing invitation to resume the old habits and the old role. "Sit by us, woman, in this moment of rest and pleasure, and entertain yourself with us, indeed entertain us. Remember that this is your vocation and that following it brings some advantages. Power has a benevolent smile for those who know how to obey, and, in the presence of so many splendid intellectual gifts, you might even get some small idea yourself."

C: Did you perhaps have one too many, Angelo?

B: You sure don't know him, Clarissa. Wine makes no difference to him, given how crazy he is by nature. At any rate, I assure you that this is his usual style.

A: There you go: the next step of this ridiculous ceremony—or shall I say this ceremony that would be ridiculous if it weren't tragic—the next step, too, is entirely obvious. The prey has taken the bait, and an instant before being thrown back into that chamber of horrors which is her everyday existence, she thoughtlessly enjoys the executioner's generous familiarity. The two have fraternized, and, strengthened by this incestuous tie, dismiss with a sneer whoever dares to suggest that they look behind the curtain, inside the closet, under this dangerously, culpably innocent appearance. If even a suspicion had flashed in the slave's mind, if there had been even a hint of a break in her life's seamless fabric, this sneer puts everything back in order, seals all the gaps, oils all the squeaking joints.

B: Now you're really going too far, Angelo, and I'm beginning to think that wine has an effect on you after all. Or are you trying to impress the girl here with this war surplus, this romantic waste? The chamber of horrors, behind the curtain, inside the closet, and maybe even under the bed. And why all this? Do you think that if I had seen a dominating male come along at this time of day, with a heavy load of books, I wouldn't have extended to him the same invitation? Wouldn't I have invited even you—only to be sorry for it a minute later?

A: Maybe, but you wouldn't have spoken the same way. Clarissa noticed that your style sounded a lot like majestic Corrado's. What she didn't notice, *and couldn't notice*, is that your assimilation of your teacher has not yet gone this far—I mean not in general, not in your normal attitude. Which means: not in the presence of other men. With them you speak as you always did, you argue directly, honestly, with no frills. Here instead, before the danger represented by this alien, fascinating being, you, while accusing me of "trying to impress the girl," can't help feeling embarrassed; you wander in a void of cultural models and communication projects, and not accidentally cling to a reassuring, fatherly figure, who makes you feel at home, gives you an illusion of control, of comfort . . .

C: Come on, Angelo. One suggests that your behavior is awkward, and you immediately launch a true bombardment of—shall we say it?—rather cheap psychological lingo. Aren't you a bit thin-skinned?

A: I'm the first to admit that my behavior is awkward. It certainly is, just like Bertoldo's or your own. I want us to avoid *denying* it, because admitting the awkwardness we *all* feel is the first step toward understanding what's behind it, what generates it. Hiding it means hiding the existence of a problem, and hence preventing its solution—a solution which could improve our lives.

B: Here goes Angelo again, ready once more to save mankind from its sins and its errors. What crusade do you want to lead today, in this heat?

A: Yes, yes, keep laughing. Nice thing, laughter. It calms, it purifies, it releases tension. Where would we be without laughter? All at each other's throats, or all psychotic. Who could endure the pervasive, obsessive stress that chokes our existence, the universe of unresolved problems surrounding our everyday activities, the irritation of other people's presence within our private space? One would end up blowing out one's brains. Whereas we laugh about it, and in this convulsive, uncontrolled trembling that shakes us from deep down and often leaves us tired and aching we forget not so much the problems, the tensions, and the irritations themselves, as rather the seriousness with which we used to look at them, the restlessness they caused us, and a great peace descends upon us—the peace of those who know that difficulties won't go away but that it's possible to live with them. So all is well, but watch out that you don't overdo it, for certain difficulties might indeed go away if they were faced in a decisive and determined manner, whereas abusing this form of relief will eventually make us live with things we might well not live with, make us afraid of tension as such, keep us at an always lower level of awareness, of participation, of autonomy . . .

C: Wait a minute, Angelo, calm down. I'm all for intensity, for seriousness, for participation, but you're going overboard. Your attitude seems more like a caricature of seriousness and commitment than like the real thing. Do you think a smile is enough to diminish a person's awareness and autonomy? Come on! The effort required by a smile, or if you will the tension released in it, is minimal, and may well allow one to keep one's balance while trying to face problems effectively. Whereas in this sort of frenzy in which you move, problems lose importance, and the suspicion arises that we're in the presence of an empty display, of a maniacal striving for omnipotence, a bit decadent and a bit childish, whose only outcome is to put you at the center of attention.

A: The suspicion is perfectly justified.

C: What do you mean?

B: He wants to make trouble for you. Surprise is always a decisive element in an attack.

C: Really?

A: Yes, in a way.

C: No, look, guys, you're wasting my time. You can play these little games by yourselves, as the frustrated and aggressive intellectuals you are. I have more useful and fun ways of entertaining myself.

A: Just a moment. You've evaluated the situation correctly. Chatting about such stupid matters is no fun, and it's not even useful, at least not in the short term: it won't help you to give a better report tomorrow. So you're entirely free to leave and do more "profitable" things. But I wouldn't want you to misunderstand our last few exchanges.

C: I'm not sure I want to understand. And I'm not sure that there is anything to understand.

A: Maybe not, but I would hate for you to leave feeling like this. So, please, give me a few more minutes, finish your wine, and let me explain those phrases you found paradoxical and irritating.

C: O.K., let's hear it. But try to be brief.

A: It will only take an instant. Look, when you say that I'm showing off, or Bertoldo says that certain rhetorical moves of mine are an attempt to make trouble for the opponent—you, in this case—it would be silly to deny that you're on target, and that part of what makes me speak, and say what I say in the way I do, is a mixture of childishness and aggressiveness. I accept all this and at the same time ask, ask *you*: "Who cares?" Who cares about my motivations? Who cares about why *this* individual says these things? Probably he says them for the wrong reasons, because he's a bit—or a lot—crazy, but let's consider for a second *what* he says, *the fact* that what he says is said, the fact that these words are uttered and that their being uttered—for whatever reason—can in turn set some mechanisms in motion, drive other individuals to make other moves, and in the end maybe even change an unacceptable state of affairs.

B: Are you now proposing the Marxist theory of the intellectual transcending his class?

A: Maybe, but with no pretense to making the intellectual a lighthouse, a guide directing others in a conscious, inspired way toward a better destiny. No, I'm convinced that you're right, that instead we wander in the darkness and say things because at the time we like saying them, because our adrenaline has reached a certain level . . .

C: No, wait, this is too easy. First *you* have a problem, you say or do things for the wrong reasons, and suddenly we all find ourselves doing what we do for the same bad reasons—at least those of us whose destiny (or punishment, if you will, but the substance doesn't change) is to lead the world beyond unacceptable states of affairs. How do you know that speaking just because you've got a mouth, or because you've got the adrenaline, is such a general way of speaking, that others don't say and do what they consider right, *because* they consider it right?

A: I have no problem admitting that things may be so. I didn't mean to make a statement of universal scope. If some people operate as you said, so much the better for them, perhaps so much the better for everyone. What I'm interested in is explaining how even an*other* kind of person, one who acts for mysterious and even perverse reasons, might—and note I'm only saying "might"—contribute in some way to an adaptive change.

C: O.K., I'll concede that. But now I must admit I can't even remember what we were talking about, or why we ended up debating this point.

B: Maybe we should fill our glasses once more, and our ideas will get clearer.

C: All right, let's fill our glasses, but don't tell me that my ideas need to get clearer. They were perfectly clear before I sat down at this table, and continue to be clear as far as I'm concerned; the only obscure thing around here is the smoke screen you guys like to build up, which seems to conceal a total void of proposals and ideas. But I'm not willing to act like the village idiot, or to give you an alibi by retreating; so I won't leave and I won't let you play with words like this. You've already wasted my time; now have the decency to give me some justification for it.

B: Well, if I remember correctly, Angelo was subtly and somewhat resentfully elaborating on the fact that I laughed.

A: Exactly, and I wanted to avoid our losing sight, by laughing, of a problem brought out clearly—as well as mercilessly—by our common embarrassment at facing a situation for which we're not culturally prepared.

C: What would that be?

A: That of dealing with a woman who likes to play the intellectual.

C: Now you're really pissing me off. There's someone else playing here—a very dangerous game, I assure you.

A: See, even this reaction signals the existence of a problem, and one that, far from being solved, is not even faced in a mature and responsible way . . .

B: Here we go with the Sunday sermon.

A: You've learned your lesson well, Bertoldo. But without the fair sex in the audience you don't perform so well.

C: Come on, guys, enough of this bitching. I told you more than once that I hate to waste time.

A: All right, so here's what I meant. There are places where you can't call somebody a "Negro" even if he *is* a Negro without starting a riot. The reason is obvious: the word "Negro" was associated for a long time with exploitation and inferiority, and no one sharing that reality likes to be reminded of it. The thing to do would be to change the reality, to eliminate the exploitation, but such a simple, radical solution is usually beyond our powers; the interests sustaining the present state of affairs are too strong.

B: This is the second time Angelo has launched into crypto-Marxist statements. Is he becoming a true revolutionary?

A: Frankly, Bertoldo, your need to assign to every sentence a precise location within *your* ideological scheme is endearing. Once more, there surfaces a need to feel at home, safe from anything unforeseen . . .

B: And on your side a need to show off at all costs, even at the cost of that minimum of coherence . . .

A: Why should coherence be desirable?

C: Can't you talk for more than one minute without going at each other?

A: Maybe not, and this is part of the problem: part of the embar-

rassment we were talking about—which is both a symptom of our difficulty and an obstacle to any serious attempt to resolve it.

C: Make yourself clearer.

A: That's what I'm trying to do. When faced by a situation like the
Negro's, I said, we should change the situation: make his life freer and
more comfortable, acknowledge and respect his rights, stop ostracizing
him in all spheres of his public and private activity. But we don't do any
of that, and probably can't do it. What we do instead is avoid using *the word*
"Negro." Which means: we avoid recognizing that there is a problem, and
blame the signal instead of the message.

C: And we should remember not to blame the bearer of bad news?

A: Precisely, and I don't see the reason for your sarcasm. There is great
wisdom in these popular sayings—a wisdom we no longer sense, just
because of how popular they are, and how familiar. With time, words lose
their grip, and repeating them is of no use. Then at some point, as now,
after reaching a conclusion with great effort, we rediscover the meaning
of an ancient proverb, and realize that that's the best way to express our
conclusion: one that was always available, but perhaps too close by for us
to truly see it.

C: This alleged intellectual farsightedness is quite interesting, but I'd
prefer to avoid further digressions. What did you mean to imply, with
your statements about Negroes?

A: Digressions have a function. They help us know each other, and
transmit our mental maps to one another: not just the road from *A* to *B*
but also what's around it, and may be useful at some later time. To return
to Negroes, however, what I wanted to do with my rather trivial example
was to direct attention to what is *beyond* and *behind* a certain irritation:
to how much the irritation prevents us from looking into things, thus
making for even more irritation in the future.

C: So, if I understand you correctly, you want to assimilate the situation
of the Negro who gets mad because they call him "Negro" to my own
when I get mad because you tell me that I am "playing" the intellectual.
And, clearly, to accept this assimilation—persuasively and diplomatically
suggested (who wouldn't want to be on the side of Negroes?) —is to have
lost already. Because Negroes, as you "appropriately" noted, *are* Negroes,
and even if this is a problem it is still a reality. Which means, by analogy,
that women really do "play" the intellectuals. It's a problem—poor souls!
—but a *real* problem. For the moment then the only true intellectuals,
the only ones who are serious about it, are men. What a pain for everyone,

especially those who—like you, I imagine—must assume such a burdensome responsibility!

B: You're beginning to realize what his strategy is.

A: What can I tell you? I'm probably the least likely person to perceive the implicit strategy of my own moves. I wouldn't be surprised if you were right, and my words served—once placed in a context that at the moment escapes me but is not for that reason less real than the one where I believe I control them—goals of repression and violence I consciously despise. But let me follow the logic of these words a little while longer, as I perceive it, and maybe we'll get something not entirely perverse from it.

C: You always have an answer ready, Angelo.

A: I thank you for the compliment and return immediately to your objection—to avoid additional criticisms for my tardiness. In your view, then, my example is badly tendentious: by putting together Negroes who rebel against their being called Negroes and women who rebel against their being considered "play" intellectuals, I would end up endorsing the latter (implicit) value judgment, that is, that women cannot be considered "true" intellectuals.

C: Precisely: that is my objection. And I'm curious to see how you defend yourself.

A: At the risk of making you mad again, I'm forced to declare that I *have no intention* of defending myself. It seems to me that you hit the bull's eye, indeed that you anticipated the conclusion of my reasoning by a few steps.

C: So it's true that you share this male-chauvinist value judgment?

A: I share the recognition that, as long as the values are the male-chauvinist ones, as long as it's males who say what an intellectual should be, as long as they dictate the rules of the game, women can only cut a poor figure: the figure of those who try to force themselves into an unnatural mold, to impose on themselves a task that others have prescribed for *their own* reasons. This is violence, too, the most subtle and possibly the most effective kind: to convince women that their liberation requires their transformation into copies of men, which means *bad* copies of men, for nothing can turn out well if it isn't natural—or at least as well as for those to whom it *is* natural.

C: I begin to see where you're going, and I must say I don't like it at all. How can you speak of naturalness, when you consider the conditions of oppression in which—as you yourself noted—women have lived so far? Don't you see that precisely yours is the subtlest form of violence, and of irony, too? Don't you see that you're cementing, with an all-too-simple reference to quasi-genetic differences, the very discrimination and segregation you were criticizing? Doesn't the true liberation of women amount to giving them the same opportunities men have always had and *waiting* while they try to overcome the inevitable conditioning caused by millennia of slavery, without cheap sarcastic remarks, without bad jokes, even with a bit of solidarity?

A: You're asking a lot of questions, and I'm not sure I have enough answers. I may have no answers at all. Let me, however, suggest one thing—not because I'm convinced that it's true but because it seems an interesting alternative and I would like for us all to think about it. I believe that, when we speak about such general—I'd like to say philosophical—things, we often run into problems of vocabulary and end up hurting ourselves, not so much because we forget the right words but because the right words do not exist, and we must invent them, and if they're not invented we keep using the old ones, and the old ones hurt. I believe we're dealing here with a problem of this kind. I said "natural," and you immediately took it in terms of the nature-nurture, genetics-environment debate, and attributed to me a well-defined— and questionable—position within that debate. But I'm not at all convinced that the debate is reasonable, and I don't want to take *any* position in it: I want to remain outside it. Still, "natural" is the only word I can find to get closer to what I mean. As a result, any attempt to express myself involves me in struggles I have no part in and whose legitimacy I don't recognize.

C: I don't understand what other sense the word "natural" could have. Get clearer.

A: I'll try. In my opinion, whether nature or nurture comes first is a pseudoproblem. Each of us has a genetic heritage that grew up originally in response to the environment and must be "completed" at the individual level by receiving information from the outside—where "outside" means both nature and culture. If the environment is modified—possibly because *we* modify it—the genetic patrimony is also likely to be modified, in the long run, and there may even come a time soon when it's possible to modify it directly, by complicated engineering techniques. But no modification will change the fact that an individual's adaptation requires the collaboration—I'd say the compenetration—of genetic and cultural factors, and certainly we'll have to be careful, if we acquire the engineering technology I was talking about, to keep the compenetration within limits that are adaptive for our species.

C: It sounds like you're reinventing the wheel.

A: I know, and in fact I haven't yet reached the point I wanted to make. But it's important to situate this point within a general theoretical horizon, and so much the better if we share the horizon: maybe we'll share the conclusions, too.

C: I doubt it.

A: I do, too, and it will be interesting to see where the disagreement arises. At any rate, within the theoretical horizon I tried to delineate, "natural" means simply this: natural for such and such an individual, in such and such a phase of its species' development, with such and such a history of adaptation—genetic *and* cultural, where the "and" is not just a conjunction but is an attempt to express the compenetration I spoke of—to the environment where that species happens to live. That is all: I make no reference to an alleged "nature" of the individual, which would remain unchanged in some Platonic heaven whatever the ecological and genetic catastrophes taking place in the area. Nor is there any attempt at castrating history, at denying future possibilities of development, at preventing individuals from acquiring different "natural" traits. At most, there's an attempt to say: look, up until now, for better or worse, we've been adaptive, but nothing assures us that we would remain so with different "natures."

C: There comes the threat. At the end of all this pseudoscientific speech comes the old, worn-out line that change is a risk which it's best not to run: revolution is a good thing but it's not for us.

A: Thank you for citing my favorite philosopher. And up to a point I agree with you: there's no threat—not that I'm aware of, at least—but certainly there's fear, which can have conservative purposes and consequences. But let's not stop at the emotional side of this thing; let's get to what I intended to be a proposal—a sincere one, in good faith—of another viewpoint, which might give us a different image of the situation.

C: Yes. Where is the "interesting alternative" we should all think about? So far I've heard nothing alternative *or* interesting.

A: You don't seem much inclined to collaboration, but once more your reactive attitude is itself part of the problem we're trying to face. So I will just go ahead and formulate my proposal, which consists in the following: instead of daydreaming about how we could or should change our present "natures," why don't we try to express and exploit all their potentialities? The reasons why women and men are different, have conflicting tendencies and intuitions, and experience difficulties in "naturally" adapting to the same tasks and projects, may well be environmental, in the last analysis, and it's entirely possible that, by modifying the environment, we might make them less different, change their "natures." But why should we? Are we sure that this uniformity won't turn against us?

C: Against you males for sure.

A: Maybe, and maybe against everyone, insofar as it limits the number of available options, of operational possibilities.

C: So say it clearly, that "in everyone's interest" it's best for women to stay home and knit.

A: This is not at all what I mean. The gender difference acts at three distinct levels. First, for reasons we're not presently concerned with, there is the pure and simple fact that certain choices and attitudes are more natural for one gender than for the other. Then come value judgments on what choices and attitudes are "better." And finally there is a power structure founded on those judgments, by which the gender having the "inferior" kind of intuitions is forced to stay home and knit.

C: You seem somewhat naive. Aren't the value judgments based on the distribution of power, rather than vice versa?

A: You may be right, but for my present purposes this complication is irrelevant . . .

C: You're really something, Angelo! Sometimes you can even admit you're wrong, as long as it's irrelevant.

A: Please don't be polemical . . .

C: Sure, no polemic. Nothing must disturb the implacable, egocentric flow of your arguments.

A: I'm not saying that. Objections are certainly legitimate . . .

C: As long as they come at the right time . . .

B: Exactly, that's how he works. Whenever you try to say something, he tells you it's not the right time, and finally, when he may have decided that the time has come, you're so exhausted that you'd rather forget it.

C: I'm beginning to understand. Our dear Angelo is really a dangerous individual.

A: If that's what you think let's indeed forget it, drink our wine and discuss the weather, or maybe go to the movies.

C: Not on your life! That way, you'd be convinced that you're not only very smart but also entirely misunderstood. No, my friend, go on and let us see where you get, but remember that you owe the time you're using more to our kindness than to your capacity for persuasion.

A: Thank you for your kindness then; I'll try not to abuse it. I meant that, even if the relation between value judgments and power structures was the opposite of the one I indicated—and in fact I'm inclined to think that you're right . . .

C: How good of you!

A: . . . it would make no difference here, because I intend to suggest precisely that we let both of these levels go. In other words, I propose that we abstract from all considerations of superiority and inferiority, *and also* (not necessarily in this order) from all the forms of constraint and violence that are often justified (*a posteriori*) on the basis of those considerations. I'll say even more: it's my opinion—as I think was clear from the beginning—that such constraint and violence are unjust and despicable, and that those value judgments are meaningless. But let's put all this aside for a moment, and concentrate on what happens at the *first* level, prior to all value judgments and power relations. Then the simplest way of saying what I mean is that this very abstraction I'm proposing contains in germ a political project—specifically a project for directing communal resources toward a common goal.

C: What goal?

A: Survival.

C: Whose survival?

A: Everyone's, what else?

C: Under what conditions?

A: The best we can achieve, and if you let me go on for a moment I'll explain what I mean.

C: O.K. Go on, tell us of this enlightened project of yours.

A: I'm not sure how enlightened it is, but at least it seems promising to me. For it seems that, if we were able to forget our ethnocentrism—where even a gender can be an *ethnos*—if we could stop regarding as negative what is only different . . .

C: Easily said.

A: So let's begin with the easy part. Let's begin by talking about it.

C: As if talking about it were of any use.

A: One starts by talking and never knows where one will end.

C: Yes, one never knows, maybe in Auschwitz.

A: What do you propose, then? Silence?

C: Forget it. Next you're going to tell me that I'm censoring your precious opinions. So, what about this political project?

A: To put it briefly, there are two distinct models of approach to reality, and there is also, unfortunately, a scale of values that determines which is better. As it is, the situation is unacceptable. To make it acceptable, we have two strategies theoretically available: we can leave the scale of values alone and assimilate the bearers of the two models, up to the point where there's only one model left, or we can reject the scale of values, reject the power structures accompanying it, and keep the diversity—which at this point would no longer be superiority or inferiority, but indeed only diversity.

C: Do you believe this is possible?

A: I believe nothing. I don't know if it's possible, and I don't know if the alternative is. I think no one does. But in such a state of uncertainty—the kind of state in which we ordinarily make our choices—it's natural for me to privilege the strategy that promises, in my view, the best results. Well, to me diversity is always advantageous, because it prepares us to face a greater number of problems, and uniformity is always disadvantageous, because it limits our operational capacities. So I prefer to invest my energies in trying to convince men and women that they're not better or worse but only different, and that instead of trying to become more and more alike they should exploit to the maximum the richness of their "models," make both their approaches as sophisticated and detailed as possible, apply them—at least as a "mental experiment"—to all the contexts they can reach, so that we all have *two* points of view available on things, on all things, *two* tools to use in facing and solving the difficulties that the environment will inevitably create for us.

C: In the abstract, what you say sounds fairly reasonable, though I still think it can't be done.

A: How do you know that the opposite can be done?

C: Now it's you who are interrupting. I *don't* know. Maybe "it comes naturally to me," to put it in your terms. But this diversity of mine seems to bother you; you seem to like diversity only when it fits *your* theoretical schemes.

A: You're right, I'm sorry. I didn't mean to sound critical.

C: The best way not to sound critical is not to be it. But let's not discuss this conflict of intuitions—indeed there isn't much there to discuss. I'd rather see you give more detail, and tell us something specific about the two tools you're talking about. What do you think distinguishes them, precisely?

A: It's not easy for me to be precise, since I possess one of them at most. But I have an idea, and no one can help me better than you to understand whether, and to what extent, it's plausible. I got it as I was studying Kant.

B: I thought it strange that old Immanuel had not yet shown up.

A: Bertoldo already knows the fundamental lines of my reading of Kant, so what I'm going to say will bore him. I'll try to be brief.

B: Famous last words!

A: On my interpretation, the essence of the Copernican revolution is this: beforehand, the concept of an object constituted the logical foundation, and every other concept—that of a person, for example, or of a mental state—had to be reduced to it, to be defined or characterized in its terms; after the revolution it's the concept of an experience that becomes fundamental, and even to explain what an object is one must begin by talking about how certain experiences are structured and integrated with one another.

C: A semantic revolution, in other words.

A: Right, and I'll spare you the rest of the story with all its complications. What I'd rather emphasize here is that, when I looked around with these two alternative paradigms in mind, and I mean—being a philosopher—looked around primarily within the history of philosophy, I began to see the same contrast everywhere, and ended up convincing myself that, whatever the historical importance of the Kantian project—enormous, as I see it—one was not to think of it as an epochal event in our process of rationalizing the world, a chasm rigidly defining two domains, a sort of conceptual discovery of America, but rather as a very strong oscillation—one of the strongest—in a pendulum movement between two extremes, which have *always* influenced our thought processes with their contrasting visions and with the tension that has *always* existed between them. And it was natural for me, since there were *two* paradigms, and one (the realist one) seemed dominant whereas the other (the idealist one) carried on an often obscure and unrecognized struggle, though not without some remarkable effectiveness—it was natural, as I said, if perhaps somewhat magical and primitive, to associate these two conceptions with the two genders, the two sexes, and to see in the lack of communication that necessarily exists between the two paradigms (for the very simple reason that they do not and cannot have a language in common) the ultimate reason for the lack of communication that seems to exist between man and woman.

C: "Magical and primitive" indeed! It sounds like we're getting down to the grossest kind of irrationalism.

A: Maybe, if you think that I want to prove the "correctness" of what I'm saying. But, as Bertoldo knows, not only do I have no such goal, but indeed I'm convinced that philosophy is constitutionally incapable of proofs like this. Its task, it seems to me, is rather to tell stories about how things *could* go, and so much the better if the stories are interesting and suggestive, if they extend our reflections instead of restricting and mortifying them, if they point to connections and relations that may look absurd at first sight, but *can* also be instructive.

C: Once more, your position is quite reasonable in the abstract but suspect in the details. When you speak in general terms, you speak of liberating thought, of telling original stories, and so on, but when you finally get to your "exemplary novel" everything sounds old and musty—worse, politically reactionary. What does this story of yours reduce to but the commonplace attribution to women of an emotional—shall we say uterine?—way of reasoning, maybe tempered by some such joke as "the heart has its reasons, which reason does not know."

A: Allow me to criticize you, for once. This objection seems based on a doubtful and, to use your own expression, somewhat "dangerous" presupposition. It appears that, just as Aristotle considered a *reductio ad infinitum* equivalent to a *reductio ad absurdum*, you think it's enough to involve me in a *reductio ad praeteritum*—if you permit me the neologism—to liquidate me. In other words, if what I say sounds like something we've already heard, like a *cliché*, then it *must* be wrong. The reason being, apparently, that ancient (so-called) wisdom accompanied the brutal exploitation of women, and hence the best strategy for detaching ourselves from that exploitation is to abandon everything associated with it. But I would like to invite you, to use another old line, not to throw out the baby with the bath. After all, there had to be something right in that "wisdom," if it let us survive and prosper until now.

C: Some more prosperously than others.

A: O.K., and yet throwing everything away might not be the best strategy. It might indeed put us all on the same level, but the lowest one. Why don't we try instead to do as the artists of the *nouvelle cuisine* do with the old recipes: purify them of what is no longer to our taste, drop the ingredients that are too rich or heavy, but keep what can still be useful and enjoyable? If the bean soup is too greasy, let's drop the grease but keep the soup. Without the metaphor . . .

B: Yes, leave out the metaphor, I'm already getting hungry.

C: I wouldn't mind some good bean soup myself.

A: What I mean is that our relation to the past shouldn't be an all-or-nothing thing: pedantic conservation or total rejection. We should rather define our goals, and then look for the most effective tools to address them. The past is a great reservoir of tools, so new goals won't necessarily mean rejection of all that was used in the past. Something, or even a lot, of what was used then can still be serviceable, and can be adapted to different ends. Specifically, rejecting the exploitation and alienation of women need not imply a rejection of all the intuitions about the female (and male) nature that accumulated and crystallized through millennia of observation and practice.

C: And what do these sacrosanct intuitions tell you: that man is rough and violent and woman tender and pretty?

A: Maybe, but I'm not forced to accept *what* they tell me. All I'm committed to is taking them seriously, and trying to discover their logic. This logic might be a deep structure, far from immediate awareness, and difficult to bring to light.

C: I'm really curious to see what you can bring to light by using these soap-opera banalities.

A: Nothing more than what I already suggested, and you already disputed. Man is supposed to have an ideal of dominion, of possession, whereas woman is supposed to be inclined to feelings, to emotional relations. And this is supposed to be the reason why the two genders misunderstand each other, why they fight and get hurt.

C: One gender more than the other.

A: I don't deny it. But you'll admit that the best thing is not to match blow for blow, but rather to ask why all this happens. Is it an obsessive, malignant fate, an original sin, an effect of God's envy? My proposal is that we're in the presence of two different conceptual schemes, which only with great difficulty can be translated into one another, so that misunderstandings are only to be expected.

C: And the incomprehension, and the violence that follows, is no one's fault.

A: That's not what I said. It might be possible—for others, since to me things are not very clear—to assess responsibility and guilt for the suffering and the injustice produced by this state of affairs. It's a common belief that, when something bad happens, someone must bear the blame for it, and I don't intend to criticize this opinion—at least not now. What I want to explore is the possibility of *changing* the state of affairs, or at least of understanding what brought it about.

C: It's easy: the desire one gender had to overpower the other.

A: That may be too easy. Once more, I don't claim to be absolutely right, but try—as an experiment—to move in a different direction, a more sophisticated one if you will. Suppose that a man reasons in terms of objects: independent, indifferent, and self-enclosed. These objects existed before him and will continue to exist, impassive like gods, after his death. They have nothing necessarily to do with him or with anything like him, no need for a consciousness to understand them and make them intelligible; they can stand perfectly well on their own. They are what they are whatever man thinks or feels. And suppose that man wants to establish some kind of relation with creatures like this, that he's not satisfied with a solipsistic, onanistic existence, but wants to reach beyond himself, overcoming the conceptual isolation to which he's condemned by his way of conceiving the world. What road can he travel in order to achieve his goal?

C: Yes, what road can he take? Poor dear.

A: That of making those objects *his own*, of controlling their accessibility and their workings, of including them within his sphere of influence, while at the same time maintaining their identity, avoiding at all costs *reducing them* to himself—which would deprive them of their status as "real" objects and would end up making the whole game not worth playing.

B: And what would be the criterion that distinguishes this form of possession from a true identification?

A: As I see it, it's legitimate to say that *A* possesses *B* only when it's possible that *something else C* has with *B* exactly the same relation *A* has. So I won't say that I *possess* a sensation of joy or a visual perception, since it wouldn't even make sense to ask whether you could possess precisely that (identical) sensation or perception. But I will say that I possess a car, or a VCR, or a slave, because in different circumstances you could have with that car, that VCR, or that unfortunate human being exactly the same relation of control I have.

B: It's interesting that it's just mental states that are not covered by this paradigm.

A: That's right. The serious problems I was suggesting are due to the fact that not only do the two genders have different paradigms, but what is the starting point in one paradigm is virtually an anomaly in the other.

C: O.K., at this point we've shed enough tears for the sad destiny of males, forced by the conceptual desert where they find themselves to build bridges here and there by making an appropriate use of their long claws and sharp teeth. Let's get to the logic of their equally unfortunate partners.

A: The word "logic" is just right, Clarissa. For we are indeed dealing with laws of thought, that is, with the general working modes of our apparatus for rationally elaborating the world.

C: Your surprise at discovering that someone else may be right is moving, or rather it would be if it weren't that being right in general means agreeing with you.

A: *Touché!* It will be better to go on. So suppose that woman reasons instead on the basis of experiences. By their nature, experiences all belong to a subject, in a different sense from the possession identified earlier but also in a sense that makes possession virtually a useless complication, since the conceptual void one tried to fill through appropriation and control doesn't exist here: experiences already arise within a general experience, are lived from a well-defined point of view, and, however informative it might be to study their specific structural relations, that they do or do not have such relations is a contingent fact, which does not modify but indeed presupposes their primordial "coexistence."

C: Very interesting, but how do you get from here to "The Bold and the Beautiful"?

A: I'm getting there. For a creature reasoning like this, isn't it natural to think that every "external" relation—that is, every relation formulated in terms of those *objects* which are the starting point of the male language —should be explained in terms of "subjective" perceptions, where this word involves no negative judgment but means only "the subject's"? Isn't it natural that the alternative paradigm's fundamental resource and preoccupation—the idea of "possession"—will be seen with puzzlement and suspicion, and hence that, on the one hand, one will not see what's so good about it and, on the other, when trying to be more conciliatory, one will try in some way to "justify" it in terms accessible to *one's own* paradigm—that is, on the basis of emotions, of experiences, of a *content* that always precedes any*thing*? Isn't it natural that this content will be structured according to its intrinsic laws and, instead of striving for a mythical adequacy to an "objective," foreign reality, will rebel against this objectivity, or at least against the attribution of central, decisive importance to it—that it will look for its own value system, based on what is "felt" as positive or negative, on what is grasped by an "intuition" often deaf to the call of "normal" perception and attentive instead to the internal coherence of the whole experiential complex: the whole of what is accepted as "real" and "plausible" as well as of what is not at all real or plausible, but still tries to come to light, to speak with a voice that can be heard by the "sensitive" soul? And, considering how different these two ways of understanding the world are, and how critical we tend to be of those who think differently from us, is it strange if the bearers of the two paradigms end up believing that the others not only do not understand them but in fact will never be able to?

C: There remains the problem of how *you* can understand all this.

A: I'm not at all sure I do. It's not by chance that you've already told me a couple of times that what I say makes more sense in general than in detail, more in the abstract than *in concreto*. I tried to make my proposal as specific and well-defined as I could, but as a philosopher I face an inevitable vagueness and lack of precision. In this role, I can only maneuver words, and even if these words "recall" things or actions, they do so in an eerie, imperfect way, and with no guarantee of coherence. The only way of really finding out how to do something is to do it. Talking about it may or may not be useful and, if it is, it's often for reasons unknown to us. So the only way to know how a woman thinks and lives is *to be* a woman, and to think and live as one; as a man, I can only tell stories about it, hoping to hit the target occasionally but with no assurance that I will.

C: You're admirably modest. But now, what would you suggest to a woman who wanted—in your terms—to thoroughly explore the potentialities of her logic?

A: I would suggest that she get started on the true conceptual revolution our species needs.

C: Which is?

A: See, feminists are right when they say that the metaphysics, the epistemology, the ethics, and the aesthetics done so far are a metaphysics, an epistemology, etc. *of men*, and that it's time to think of building a feminine variant of them. But one must be careful not to misunderstand this need, which the feminists occasionally seem to do. Take metaphysics, for example. There is metaphysics in general, and there is special metaphysics: say, the metaphysics of elementary particles or living tissues. And note that, when I say "the metaphysics of elementary particles," the genitive in this phrase must be understood as an objective one. The metaphysics *of* elementary particles, in other words, is the metaphysics *that deals with* elementary particles. Well, just as there is a metaphysics of elementary particles, there is of course a metaphysics of people and—why not?—of men and of women. In these last few cases, however, the genitive can also be understood as a subjective one: the metaphysics of people can also be a metaphysics *done by* people, and analogously for the metaphysics of men and women.

C: Thank you for this learned statement.

A: I apologize for what may sound like pedantry, but the distinction is extremely important. The fact is that quite often, when one tries to construct an alternative to the classical "male" metaphysics, one ends up with a metaphysics "of women" *where the genitive is understood as objective*. That is, with a metaphysics that categorizes women, that explains their general properties, that reveals their essence, just as it might reveal the essence of mice or electrons. And *this* kind of metaphysics, I believe, is not at all an answer to the traditional one, primarily because it requires no responsibility on women's part: it could very well be done by men, examining a gender foreign to them with the same detachment with which they examine other animals.

C: And with the same inability to understand it, unless women intervene to explain.

A: Maybe, and hence the fact that women are intelligent animals, with whom one can establish a dialogue and from whom one can get verbal data, is certainly a great advantage. But remember that no data are irrefutable, and hence a metaphysics *of women* in this sense could well conclude that *all* of women's intuitions about women are mistaken. At any rate, if the feminist program went no further, if all there were to it were the claim that women's opinions must be important or even decisive when speaking of women, it would reduce to a parochial pronouncement, which might possibly cure some old injustices but certainly would not let us profit much from what women can say and do. What we need instead is a metaphysics of women in the *subjective* sense: we need metaphysical systems based on the intuitions proper to women, on their way of thinking, and we need to throw these systems into the arena together with the "male" ones, so that they contribute to giving us new, interesting points of view on all there is. I don't want to know, or at least I don't want *only* to know, what women think *of women*: I also want to know what they think of men, of elementary particles, and of living tissues, what all of these things look like in their eyes. And I want to know—going beyond metaphysics now—what their ethical and aesthetic judgments are, their ideas about knowledge, their positions concerning skeptical dilemmas.

C: Do you believe that these positions and judgments would be substantially different, not just in detail but in their general structure, in their methodology, from those elaborated by male philosophy?

A: I can't say, I don't feel I know enough to express a sensible opinion. But I certainly hope that they would be—because of how much this feminine perspective might teach us, enrich us, surprise us. And I hope so for women themselves: I hope their liberation doesn't run out of gas too soon, that it won't be restricted to giving them a little more room in a world that remains men's because it's *thought* by men. I hope that, side by side and in competition with this one, there will arise a world of women, too—which doesn't mean made of women or controlled by women but rather born out of a feminine project, a hypothesis, a plan that men couldn't even conceive.

C: In other words . . .

A: In other words, returning to the distinction between subjective and objective, what I want is a woman who becomes a subject of history, who no longer looks on herself and her gender as something to be manipulated on the basis of an alien logic, but rather imposes *her own* logic on history, becomes a protagonist of it, and possibly takes it in a new direction, which at the moment we can't predict.

B: Wait a minute, Angelo: let me play the devil's advocate.

A: Be my guest. I couldn't wait to hear your voice again.

B: I've been quiet so far because, all things considered, Clarissa was standing up to you well, but now I notice that—with great skill, I should say—you've started riding the feminist bandwagon.

A: I'd rather say "feminine."

C: And you would be right. Indeed . . .

B: Whatever, as you prefer. This very exchange, on the other hand, is a good example of what worries me. Feminism, or the feminine, is fashionable, and like all fashionable phenomena it has its set of passwords, the Open Sesames that unlock all doors and overcome all resistances. You know these passwords very well, as I can see, and—what's worse—use them shamelessly.

A: Still another attack on my integrity. Some day we'll have to face this problem, Bertoldo.

B: You're right, some day we will. In this case, however, I said "worse" without referring to your moral stature. I was referring to the danger caused by your very ability: the danger of not understanding each other just because we believe we understand too well, of being seduced by trendy words while forgetting the choices those words commit us to, perhaps against our interests.

C: Now it's you who must get clearer, because . . .

B: Yes, I know: I wasn't very clear. Angelo was right when he said that it's difficult to speak about certain things, in certain situations, and that because it's difficult one tends to act like a fool. But now I've decided that, however difficult, the subject is too important to be dismissed with a pun; so, even if it costs me and I don't perform at my best, I will make my contribution.

A: We appreciate your spirit of sacrifice very much.

B: See, Angelo, there are obvious reasons for your triumphant attitude. As usual, you presented a strange position, got negative reactions to it at first, but were eventually able to articulate it and justify it in a credible and convincing way. You were good, my congratulations.

A: Thank you, you're too kind . . .

B: No, not *too* kind. Those are the only kind words I feel like saying to you. For, after noticing your skill, I immediately pose the following question: what's the point of it? For example, you now use the plural, you say, "we appreciate very much," and I ask myself who is included in this plural.

A: It's really grammar's day: earlier I spoke about genitives and now you speak about numbers.

B: Yes, and in both cases grammar seems to have a deep ideological significance. By using the plural you suggest a common position, and because you use the first person plural it must be a position you share. So I ask: Share with whom? What community are you referring to?

A: In this case, clearly, the "community" formed by myself and Clarissa.

C: Who on the other hand . . .

B: Of course, but the "deep" logic of your discourse intimates other, wider associations: you also speak in women's name, or maybe in the name of the women who rise to become protagonists of history, or of the whole human tribe. Perhaps you're speaking in my name, too.

A: I wouldn't go that far.

B: Because I'm not enough of a protagonist? Jokes aside, my problem is as follows: your position has very little plural character, very little that is common, and *presenting* it as common, by using the plural, is a subtle form of misrepresentation.

A: Here we go again, Bertoldo. What are you accusing me of now, intellectual malpractice? I sure am full of vices.

B: No, look, I'm not making a moral judgment; we'll discuss your morals some other time. Right now I'm not interested in knowing how consciously responsible you are for what I consider a mistake: I'm only interested in emphasizing that it is a mistake.

A: What mistake?

B: In a certain sense, the same for which I've blamed you on other occasions. And you'll tell me that calling it a "mistake" implies a value judgment, that I should limit myself to speaking of diversity, that I'm ethnocentric, and so on. But, if you let me put it my own way, you're simply making a big mistake.

A: Then correct me. I'm at your disposal.

B: I don't believe I can correct you, and I'm not sure that I *want* to correct you; after all, what you think is not so important, at least not *because* you think it. But if I believe that it's wrong I must fight against it, and try to prevent it from becoming *more* important and conquering others.

A: Here we're finally beginning to do things for real: philosophy as a boxing match.

B: Don't delude yourself: you're aggressive, too. You just have your own style, which may well be a more effective one. But you are aggressive, no doubt about it, and enjoy winning a debate like anyone else, maybe more than anyone else.

A: If I remember correctly, you said you didn't mean to discuss my horrible sins.

B: O.K. So let's get to the point. As far as I'm concerned, your mistake is that you always move in a universe of words, as if this universe were entirely self-sufficient. Specifically, you don't seem to be troubled by the fact that there are also *things*, and words might make sense because they're associated with them. Of course, since you're not new to this game, you also have a theoretical position that justifies your practice—that "rationalizes" it, to use a term you like. Upon request, you can deliver a long story concerning how practices follow their blind, unpredictable course, and the stories we tell about them will remain forever suspended in midair, so that, if indeed they must remain suspended, let's at least make them form some beautiful figures, let's turn them into kites.

A: The next thing I know you'll become a poet.

B: It's all because of the example I've been set, Angelo, primarily by you. So in the past we discussed this position of yours and got to a dead end: you have your ideas, I have mine, you develop yours, I develop mine, the world is beautiful in its variety. But, frankly, I don't like this dead end. Variety is not necessarily beauty: a variety of extermination techniques, to put it in somewhat excessive terms . . .

A: I wouldn't say "somewhat" . . .

B: Then *very* excessive terms. Excess makes things clearer sometimes. Well, a variety of this kind wouldn't generate any aesthetic delight in me.

A: Your robust moral sense must get into it, one way or another.

B: Probably. I must be stuck at the ethical stage, as Kierkegaard would say. Be that as it may, our present discussion seems a perfect example of our lack of communication, and might help us overcome the dead end, or at least face it constructively. You claim that it would be desirable for women to raise more than a simple demand for their share of power, freedom, and happiness—a demand I too consider only right. What you want is something much more radical: a different way of thinking of the world, the abandonment of a conceptualization of experience in terms of objects to be appropriated, a universal, extraordinary turnabout of the whole logic used so far. These are nice words: here, around a table, at the margins of productive life, with a glass of wine in front of us . . .

A: Incidentally, mine is empty.

B: . . . it's fun to talk like this. Which may be enough for you: you believe that an intellectual is always at the margins of productive life, that his only purpose is chattering, and that there is no connection between his chattering, or anybody's, and action, the real process of transformation of the world.

A: You learned the lesson well.

B: I had a good teacher. But I don't believe in this separation between theory and practice, indeed I consider it dangerous and immoral . . .

A: Here we go with immorality again.

B: Yes, immoral, if not intentionally then at least in its objective consequences. The stories we have told so far, whether male-chauvinist or not, have made it possible for us to live very well, and have freed us to a great extent from the humiliating, bestial labor by which our ancestors provided for their needs. We've gained a lot, much more than was legitimate or reasonable to hope for, and now we might want to distribute all this more equitably, to give women what they have a right to—and not only women, but also for example the inhabitants of developing countries or the many unfortunate people who, even in the West, have fallen by the wayside. But, just when it's time to open up the party, to share the cake that only a few have enjoyed so far, you come up with these spoiled intellectual's demands and, instead of offering women fairness and justice, ask them for a new toy to play with, a new tale before bedtime. You don't give a damn about the practical implications of your choice, for you're convinced that tales have no such implications, but do you think that they—those very women you include in your first person plural—that they like to be told: "Forget about the life of privilege *we* lived so far. Let's throw everything overboard and start again, with a new approach, a revolutionary, feminine logic. Indeed, come to think of it, why don't *you* elaborate this new approach while we continue to enjoy the situation, since diversity is valuable anyway and it's best for everyone if male and female approaches confront each other in a creative way"?

A: Your verbal fury is impressive, and I must say I'm a bit embarrassed by it. But I don't want to avoid your questions and the challenge they entail; so I won't limit myself to the obvious point that everyone has a right to his opinion, and will try instead to face what you correctly called a dead end.

B: A promising beginning.

A: If I understand you correctly, your criticism is more or less of the following sort. The approach I attributed to males—that is, the one that sees the world in terms of objects to be appropriated and about which to legislate—has paid extraordinary dividends. It's given us television and the airplane, let us reach the moon, extended our lives, helped us overcome labor and hunger. So at this point it's useless and irresponsible to ask women for an*other* approach, before they have had an opportunity to enjoy their share of the advantages of *this one*. The current attitude has proved its adequacy through its successes; therefore the right thing to do, instead of thinking of an improbable alternative, is to make those successes available to a larger part of mankind.

B: You understood perfectly well. Now answer.

A: Take it easy. I realize you feel you have the upper hand, and can't wait to strike the killing blow; but your knife may be blunt. Undeniably, in the last three centuries, progress, so-called, took off and produced impressive results. It's difficult to set a beginning for this "mad race"; one might find it in the industrial revolution, or in the discovery of the calculus, or even further back, in that extraordinary concentration of brains which came together in the Florence of the 1400's.

B: You're taking the long way around.

A: Why not? You raised a theme of global import, so it's right to situate it within an equally wide perspective.

B: As long as we don't get lost in it.

A: Let's hope not. Philosophy, as usual slow but sure in siding with the winner, took a couple of centuries, more or less, to theorize the new model of "understanding" on which this technical-practical turnabout was based. The theorization was explicitly formulated for the first time in the *Critique of Pure Reason*.

B: Kant must always get into it somehow.

A: Yes, but you'll see that this time he doesn't play the hero. In the Preface to the *Critique*, Kant identifies the characteristic element of the new attitude. It's this: instead of remaining a passive spectator of natural occurrences, man assumes direction and control. He asks definite questions of nature, and manipulates it according to his parameters and projects. He understands more because he *does* something, and he understands primarily *what he does*.

B: Well, Kant was not the first to formulate this position. It's an ancient theme.

A: Yes, but there's something more in Kant: a precise reference to the experimental method. It's this method that put physics onto the road of science, he thinks, and philosophy must imitate it if it wants to have the same success. And what's the fundamental characteristic of this method?

B: You just said it: the assumption of an active attitude.

A: Let's go into more detail. Experiments are carried out *in a laboratory*, that is, in an artificial situation, created by man for his own purposes. In a laboratory, the experimenter exercises enormous power. The dimensions of variability of phenomena are completely subject to his plans: he makes a (limited) number of parameters interact and studies the consequences of this interaction.

B: What's wrong with that?

A: So far, nothing. Inside the laboratory, man not only feels but also *is* godlike. The environment was tamed quite effectively, and the surprise element reduced to a minimum. One ends up finding what one was looking for, and hence what one *expected* to find: it's only a question of time, commitment, and funds.

B: Wait a minute: you were the one who used the metaphor of the lab to indicate the proper place for conceptual revolutions to be carried out—revolutions which, as you also said, are the more effective the crazier they are. How can you now assert that what happens in a lab is expected and predictable?

A: If you think about it, it isn't so strange. Making the lab the revolutionary place *par excellence* means, as we said on another occasion, freezing revolution and revolutionaries, separating them from empirical reality, condemning them to isolation. The lab as such—as a structure man creates to conduct his play without risk—gives expression to precisely the opposite demand from revolution: a demand for control, verification, and caution. True revolution occurs outside the lab.

B: But science and scientists are important outside, too!

A: Sure, so it's time to consider the following step, where one tests the utility of experiments and labs by applying the results obtained there to the "real" world.

B: I don't see how this application could create problems. The situations realized in a lab are merely stylized representations, if you will, of specific real situations. So it's sufficient to apply the results obtained in the lab to real situations that are similar.

A: I have the impression that things are not so easy, and to explain what I mean I'll begin with an example. Did you ever take a logic course?

B: Yes, I even taught a few.

A: Perfect, so you know that in such courses one encounters serious difficulties when moving from the calculus' blissful, elegant abstractness to *using* the calculus in analyzing ordinary language arguments.

B: True: often students don't understand.

A: The problem is precisely what is meant by "understanding." At the beginning, students have a lot of fun: all those vertical and horizontal lines, all those formulas, all those inference rules remind them of a puzzle, a complicated mental exercise. But then they realize, or they are told, that formulas represent sentences of natural language, and that a proper use of the rules will allow them to decide things of great practical importance: say, whether they should believe the conclusions reached by a certain politician, or if they should buy a certain car or a certain after-shave.

B: What's the matter with that? It's an obvious case of applying an abstract model to concrete reality.

A: That's right: an obvious case. So if difficulties arise it's possible that they invest the whole project of this application.

B: I haven't yet seen any difficulty.

A: And you may continue not to see them. The way you put it earlier ("students don't understand") represents an attempt at avoiding them, at not acknowledging their existence. I, on the other hand, see some difficulties, indeed I see an enormous one: the ordinary language that should constitute the field of application of the "abstract" logical system doesn't resemble this system at all.

B: Sure, ordinary language is much less precise.

A: Yes, "less precise." One also says "more vague," and both expressions clearly amount to value judgments. Ordinary language is no good, doesn't "come up to" the formal model, must be improved, made clearer, "regimented" to get it as close as possible to that model. Sometimes it's little things, like saying that there is no "logical" difference between a "but" and an "and," and sometimes things get very complicated, as with quantifiers or modalities, and one faces heated debates on how the regimentation is to be carried out.

B: Once more, I don't believe there is anything strange about those debates. The parties involved represent different theories concerning the logical structure of natural language, so it's right and understandable that they should compete with each other.

A: I know you see nothing strange about it. Your position has strategies available to make these problems harmless. Still, articulating what *for me* are difficulties helps me clarify my ideas, so let me go on a little longer.

B: Take your time.

A: Leaving value judgments aside for a moment, the substance of the situation seems to be the following: formal language and natural language are *different*, and in order to apply the one to the other we must *modify* the latter. But there's no criterion telling us how far it's legitimate to carry the modifications. Of course, if we go *too* far with them, the game becomes a little trivial, and we may end up applying the formal language to itself. The only defense against such excesses is constituted by something fleeting and controversial: the so-called "intuitions" of the native speaker, which theoretically should guide us in establishing the equivalences needed for the regimentation process. And here arises the problem of the students "who don't understand." They don't understand where to stop in this process. They don't seem to have the required intuitions, so we say that they must "refine" them—and, note, refine them precisely by familiarizing themselves with the formal system and using it constantly. At the end of the course, in general, most of them are perfectly well refined; but how do we know that they haven't just got used to the system, that being forever involved with it they can no longer think in any other way, and instead of an education in logical analysis they've received a subtle form of conditioning?

B: I don't understand the question. Doesn't every form of education condition one to respond in an adequate way to certain environmental demands?

A: Maybe so. But consider the kind of conditioning I'm referring to here. Once trained, the student learns to live in a formal universe, which means: a universe "rigorously" defined by men. All that in ordinary language could betray these rigorous definitions was eliminated: being considered a symptom of roughness and imperfection, it was ruthlessly put aside and replaced with more "precise" formulas. From a casual aggregate of historical accidents, from a tortuous sedimentation of fossils coming from the most diverse strata, from a possible source of wonder and amazement, the world has become an orderly, perfectly controllable structure. But at what cost? How does it differ from one of those toy houses kids make with their building blocks?

B: And what if it doesn't? After all, language is a human creation.

A: You're right. But I was only considering an example, meant to help you—if you were so inclined—to take the steps needed to see things from my point of view. If it's certainly improper to call a set of linguistic expressions "a world," as I just did, it's also true that there is a remarkable resemblance between the conditioning perpetrated during a logic course and the "experimental" methodology in dealing with the world—the real world, this time—that we were talking about earlier.

B: Let's see this resemblance, and hope that the digression was worth it.

A: Initially, the world is complicated and obscure. Great attention and sensitivity seem needed to understand it. But here come the supporters of the "new science," proposing a wholly revolutionary attitude. Instead of looking at the world as it is, and maybe getting confused by its complexity, let's construct little abstract models of it "inside a glass ball" —"abstract" in the precise sense that they *abstract* from a number of "irrelevant" aspects of concrete reality and "concentrate" on what at the moment "is of interest" to us.

B: I don't see the reason for your sarcasm

A: I hope I can make you see it, though it's not sarcasm, only skepticism. Once this abstraction is made, the scientist can operate with his models more or less as the logician does with his systems. But at some point the problem arises of justifying this operation, and then the scientist faces the same difficulty that already troubled the logician: just as natural language doesn't much resemble a formal system, the real world doesn't have much in common with the artificial structures created in a lab. It continues to be complicated and obscure, and, if the scientist wants to apply his results to it, he must carry out once more a process of regimentation.

B: You're not suggesting that the scientist lives in a world he's himself created?

A: Not exactly. The world is more resistant than language, and hence replacing its most recalcitrant aspects with more yielding ones is not a promising strategy, at least not to begin with—since the final outcome of the whole program ends up coinciding, as I'll try to show you, with a normalization of this kind. But let's go one step at a time.

B: It sounds like a great idea.

A: What I'm saying is certainly a bit confused: there are too many things involved. But, returning to how the scientist regiments the world, I would say that, at first, this operation has the status of a wager.

B: *À la* Pascal, maybe.

A: In a way, yes, except that God is not involved. One wagers that the world is indeed similar to the artificial reality studied in the lab, so that the techniques tested in manipulating this reality will have the same success when applied to the vast *mare ignotum* to be found outside the lab.

B: Aren't you flaunting your originality when you use the word "wager"? You're saying nothing substantially new—nothing different for example from what others express by talking about "hypotheses."

A: You're right: there's a sense in which we mean the same. But the word "wager" lets me underline an element that is often missed when using neutral and dignified terms like "hypothesis": the element of *risk*. This wager has deep practical implications, it deeply influences a man's behavior—whether he's a scientist or not. It calls our very existence in question and threatens to reduce it to chaos.

B: Let me stop you before you get too biblical, and ask you to come down to earth.

A: O.K., though what I'm saying does have biblical aspects, and perhaps we shouldn't be afraid to use a certain tone when the matter requires and deserves it. At any rate, the point is as follows. The reality around us, however obscure it may be, must have its own mechanisms of self-control and self-defense because, independently of our intervention, it tends to maintain itself more or less identically, if not always then at least for rather long periods of time (at least at our scale). It's a system of great complexity but also great resilience, capable of absorbing destabilizing influences and of resisting even considerable solicitations. It might not be the best possible reality (if it even makes sense to speak like that), but certainly it's a solid, integrated one.

B: Integration is not necessarily a good thing.

A: On this point we should get clearer. In some cases it is (or seems to be) advisable to move from a state A to a state B, and for this purpose the integration present in A must be broken. But the goal of this "revolutionary" operation, one must remember, is eventually to reconstitute a *new* integration. Disintegration as such, revolution as an end in itself, doesn't seem a credible ideal to me, except perhaps in that specialized sector of reality where intellectuals belong.

B: Thus we return to your strange mixture of "institutional" fascism and "philosophical" rebelliousness.

A: Yes, and I don't think we need to debate that question once again. I'd rather emphasize the difference between the reality I described and the typical situation occurring in a lab. In a lab one acts primarily to *change* things. The lab is, as the alchemist's cabinet once was, the place where one plays out dreams of a better world, which means, among other things: a *different* world. One doesn't go into a lab without hopes of making human life something new, something that, to a small or large extent, has not existed yet, has not yet been seen. One doesn't go in there without a project, small or large, of reformation, of rebirth, of catharsis . . .

B: O.K., O.K., I got it. Let's go on.

A: I apologize for insisting on this point, but it's the key to the whole matter. Summing up, then, while the world is characterized by a tendency to balance and repetition, the ideology of the man-scientist, which after all dominates contemporary society, is one of change—change for the better, of course, but still change.

B: And would this be the biblical risk you were talking about?

A: Not directly, but it gets there pretty soon. To be precise, it gets there when one begins to realize the ideal, the dream the lab expresses—when one begins to use the results of the lab work to act outside the lab, and is inevitably led to look at the world as a gigantic lab, to adopt toward it the attitude and practices typical of the "experimental" scientist.

B: What would be so dangerous about those practices?

A: What's dangerous is that in a lab one tends to vary all the parameters one can, to see what happens. Not too many parameters are present and active there, since the situation is (as I said) an artificial one, but still variations often have vast consequences. If the lab is a closed system, however, they don't usually cause disasters.

B: Sometimes they do.

A: Sure, when the system is not closed and reactions extend beyond it. Then indeed there are risks not just for the experimenter but for the whole community surrounding him—which is often unaware of what's going on. But now try to imagine how much more serious this very problem becomes when the whole world is treated like a lab, and in the hope (or with the excuse) of making it better one constantly challenges its equilibrium and generates destabilizing influences.

B: It looks like these "destabilizing influences" were of some use.

A: Maybe, but then again maybe not. Indeed, to be frank, I rather think not. The reason why you think otherwise, and many others with you, is that you reason at a temporal scale different from mine. You say: It's been centuries by now since mathematics, physics, and so on "entered upon the sure path of science," and since then progress has been unstoppable and its results have accumulated in a solid, safe way. The resulting situation is so much better than the previous one.

B: Why? Isn't that true?

A: I don't know how it *is*. I can tell you how I see it. I tend to think of what has happened in the last three or four centuries as an episode, interesting of course but certainly not definitive, in the sense that it's not at all clear how it will end up. Dinosaurs might have thought (if they thought at all) that their situation was well established; after all, they had been around for over a hundred million years. But at some point the system varied beyond their capacity for adaptation and the planet was littered with their skeletons. And dinosaurs had change thrust upon them: they didn't play with it.

B: I would subscribe—as a species, I mean—to sticking around for another hundred million years.

A: I'm sure you would, but I don't think we'll be given the chance. For during the episode we're talking about things have moved at increasing speed, and have gotten by now to extremes of paroxysmal frenzy. Whereas you find it natural to think that, once a better world is generated, it will continue to exist indefinitely, I on the other hand believe that *under the illusion* of generating a better world we've set in motion a mechanism that has now reached its limit, and is ready to explode along with all of us, or maybe to bury us under our waste.

B: But these are conventional complaints about technology and pollution. Aside from the fact that I don't share them, and in fact consider them politically ambiguous attacks on the project of improving our lives through a rational use of our resources and creativity, I don't yet see the connection between all this and the speech—and promises—you made a little earlier. How does this third-rate ecologism and catastrophism fit with that other tale, in my view just as ambiguous, concerning the male and female paradigms?

A: I'm getting there. The myth guiding and informing the historical episode of the new science is that of *homo faber*, where incidentally it's not at all by chance that it is *homo* who is *faber*. But let's take things in the right order. According to this myth, man is primarily an *artificer*, a creature that realizes his destiny by *producing* objects—and possibly other creatures like himself—that didn't exist before. It's the myth of Hephaistos, who uses the magical fire to make weapons and utensils; it's the myth of Prometheus, who steals that fire to pass on to men the power of *making* what doesn't exist yet . . .

B: O.K., let's go on.

A: The fundamental point is that there is, I'd say, an elective affinity between this myth of the man-artificer and the male paradigm I discussed earlier: the one that conceives the world as beginning from the notion of an object.

B: Make yourself clearer.

A: I'll try. I said that it's natural, when one thinks in terms of objects, to see our relation to them primarily as appropriation. Objects are conceptually separated from us by the void of their independence, and to fill this void we tend to stretch out our hands and make objects our own. Stretch out our hands in a literal sense—and here the problem becomes a political one, the problem of how to *distribute* these objects—or in a figurative sense, appropriating objects by grasping them in thought, by uncovering their workings, by subjecting them to "scientific" laws.

B: "Subjecting" seems too strong, for the laws are not invented by us. Objects obey these laws on their own.

A: You're right. I got carried away and gave implicit expression to some personal opinions.

B: Not that implicit. It's always best with you to go very very slowly.

A: Yes, and it's good for you to watch me so closely. What I meant, however, is that it's the same need for domination and control that manifests itself both at a physical level, by trying to bring certain objects within our sphere of influence, and at an intellectual one, by discovering or inventing their laws. It's the same conceptual isolation that one wants to defeat, making *one's own* what to begin with is by definition *other than oneself.*

B: A less romantic way to put it might be that understanding things helps in dominating them—and in dominating those who want to appropriate them.

A: Sure, but it's not strange that there should be more than one sense in which the male paradigm "forces" an attitude of intellectual appropriation. One should expect that connections as important as this one are overdetermined.

B: O.K., but how do we get to the *homo faber?*

A: We'll get there right away. If the carrier of this paradigm is naturally inclined to intellectual control and domination (in addition to—or possibly as a means to—physical control and domination), he will be ontologically most "reassured" when the object is his own creation. He himself generated it, so no one knows better than he does what the nature of this object is: the object can't escape him.

B: Maybe, but the whole thing sounds contradictory. First you say that in this paradigm objects are distant and independent, and then you end up identifying its ideal with a situation where objects are *produced by* the subject himself, and hence in the last analysis neither distant nor independent.

A: Right, but what seems a contradiction to you is merely a natural dialectic. It's just *because* objects are remote and indifferent to begin with that one tries to overcome their remoteness by changing the deal, that is, by finding objects a bit closer, a bit less indifferent. And it's natural to think that these closer objects might be found in what the subject himself *has* or *has made*. Mistaken, probably, since there's no assurance that something born from us or belonging to us should in some metaphysical sense *depend* on us—think of a parent's desperation when the children leave, or of a dying miser who's going to lose his "stuff"—but natural nonetheless: a natural conviction (or shall we say delusion?) that what is ours should be so in more than an ephemeral way, that it should forever bear our traces, that it should always be possible to read of us there, to find a sign of our being and our fate.

B: Wait a minute; before you return to your inspired tone let's try to sum up with at least a minimum of clarity. According to the male paradigm, you're saying, the conceptual starting point is the notion of an object—by which we mean an object independent of the subject, of his experiences, and also of any other object, in the precise sense that its nature must not be characterizable, or definable, on the basis of the subject's nature, of the nature of his experiences, and so on. At this point, on your view, there would arise a true isolation, not only conceptual but also emotional: these "alien" objects, separated from us by an unfillable "logical void" and as such not "reducible" to us, would create a situation of uneasiness, to which one would respond by trying to appropriate them——both at a physical level, by putting one's hands on them, and more subtly at an intellectual level, that is, by getting to know them and hence by reconstructing them. So, though you think it's ultimately delusive, it would be natural for a carrier of the male paradigm to assume a "productive" attitude toward the world—that is, to assimilate it to one of the models or toys he himself dominates and manipulates in the lab—with all the (according to you, disastrous) consequences of this attitude.

A: Perfect. Your summary is tremendously lucid.

B: Thanks, and your rambling is not without consistency. Except on one point, on which I would ask you to be more explicit.

A: Bertoldo, if you didn't exist one would have to invent you. Where would I get without your careful, confident guidance?

B: Probably farther. But the problem is this: why is the conceptual void accompanied by psychological uneasiness? Why shouldn't the carrier of this paradigm just relax before an obvious and ineliminable feature of his way of thinking? Why should he make such an effort to overcome this feature?

A: Your question is right on target, as usual. But one can only give it a partial answer, for it's impossible to deal adequately with all the general problems it involves, unless we want to stay up all night.

B: There isn't much night left. But anyway, try to give us at least some idea of the situation.

A: O.K. So let's begin from the end and proceed by big steps. Take first of all what you called uneasiness, which could also be called anxiety. What does this emotional state indicate? Following a Freudian line of interpretation, I would say: a fragmentation of personality. According to the model elaborated in *Inhibitions, Symptoms and Anxiety*, the first situation that generates this kind of response is birth, when the organism is invaded by an enormous amount of energy it can't control. Then, step by step, this energy is "bound" and an Ego gets constituted, but, every time the Ego's integrity is threatened by a new invasion, anxiety is used as a signal to bring out the defense mechanisms and respond to the attack.

B: Thank you for your little lecture, but what's the relevance of the Ego and its integrity to the objects we're talking about?

A: Don't worry: the relevance is there, or so I think. Because, see, my model is not simply Freudian . . .

B: I'd be surprised if it was simply anything.

A: Exactly: what's most fun is mixing ideas, models, projects . . .

B: Never mind whether they fit.

A: They won't fit as long as *you* don't make them fit. One needs . . .

B: Yes, I know, one needs a panderer, and you seem just right for the part. But go on.

A: I thought it was strange that you hadn't come up with any moralizing remarks yet. But let's not get distracted. Going back to Freud, what I think we must dispense with is the purely quantitative analysis on which his proposal is based.

B: An analysis typical of the positivism that had so much influence on his thought.

A: Right, but still an analysis that can be emancipated from this positivist conditioning, at the cost of some complications.

B: Why don't we just forget about it, instead?

A: Because there are many instructive things in it. The Ego as the level of integration of personality, anxiety as first a response to, and then a signal of, a threat to this integration: all this makes a lot of sense to me.

B: So where's the problem?

A: The problem is that these processes—integration and *dis*integration—shouldn't be analyzed only in terms of the organism's, or the Ego's, capacity for binding energy. Energy must probably be bound, or there wouldn't be any available, but it must be bound *around something*, which can't itself be energy.

B: So what is it?

A: It's a story, a narrative, a tale, concerning how, *what* the Ego is.

B: Now you've lost me.

A: I mean that the Ego is born within a confabulation, where, among many possible *essences*, one is chosen, and becomes the point of aggregation for the *object* Ego. After this choice, the Ego can answer the classical question *ti esti?*, can say that it knows its own nature, can say what it's looking for and why.

B: Just a moment, didn't you say some other time that stories are not important, that they're neither true nor false? And now you're telling me that without a story there wouldn't even be a subject!

A: Be careful. I did say that stories, *these* stories at least, are neither true nor false, but I didn't infer from this that they're not important. Indeed I claimed that the *a posteriori* rationalization they provide calms us down, brings us peace, and now you can see better why. The stories concerning the Ego are neither true nor false—at least not in the traditional sense in which truth is correspondence with something preexisting, since in this case there's nothing preexisting to correspond with. These stories *constitute* the Ego: before they're told there's no Ego for them to describe, and afterwards they're true only in an entirely trivial, immaterial sense. The traditional categories of truth and falsity lose their relevance here, but that doesn't mean the stories are not important. Maybe it's those categories that were overvalued, and should now lose some importance.

B: I begin to realize the chaos I'm getting involved in. Let's try to collect our thoughts. Admitting that you're right about this connection between the Ego and the stories, and the previous one between the (threatened) disintegration of the Ego and anxiety, how do we get from stories to objects?

A: We get there by inquiring about the stories' nature. How are these stories constructed? Is it possible to tell a story where a single character acts in a void? No, a story needs more than one character; indeed, every story comes to life more or less explicitly as a dialogue, as a confrontation among different realities, for it's only through confrontation and diversity that each character, including the subject, can identify himself. "What am I?" refers inevitably to "what am I *not*?", to "what am I in contrast with, in opposition to?" Thus the story of the Ego gets inextricably linked with the story of the *non*-Ego, the determination of the subject's nature becomes one and the same with the determination of what's other than the subject, and man, before he can be *faber*, must become *fabulator*: a *homo theoreticus* who, to exist as such, needs to narrate and understand himself, and hence to narrate and understand the world.

B: And here comes the conceptual void?

A: Exactly! For note: one does need an *other*, in relation to and in contrast with which to define the self, but this other must not be *too much* of an other, he must not be wholly indefinite, mysterious, obscure. The encounter with the other must be something more than the "encounter" between two celestial bodies: a simple crossing of blind, silent orbits. There must be communication, there must be intellectual contact, there must be what Kant called "affinity" between subject and object: a responsiveness, a resonance between the laws of thought and the laws of being. A responsiveness and resonance that, as Kant himself remarked, are entirely inaccessible within the realist logical scheme we're discussing.

B: So the realist ends up a schizophrenic?

A: Not schizophrenic, at least not necessarily. I'd say unbalanced, that is, always trying to prove to himself the correctness of his stories through a manifestation of control and domination. Since initially the world is foreign to us, we'll make it *our own*, and to convince ourselves that it *is* our own we'll continue to manipulate it, to play with it as a child plays with a doll or with Lego, to change it according to our wishes and plans—trying to overcome with all this frantic motion the doubt, the suspicion that always lies in wait, that always threatens us: the doubt, the suspicion that we're still not getting anywhere.

B: And you think that the feminine paradigm would have no such problems?

A: It might have others, but not these ones. For there objects would be at most a destination—if indeed one ever arrives there—and the starting point would be different. One would think of the world starting from one's own experiences: there would be no voids to fill, foreign realities to conquer, alien individuals to bring back to the laws of our Ego. One would rather have to follow with close attention the structuring of these experiences, lend an ear to their voices, watch them as they respond to each other, as they unroll and articulate themselves, and possibly as they thus constitute—temporarily or permanently—objects "distinct" from us.

B: Do you mean that this paradigm goes together naturally with a passive, contemplative attitude?

A: Yes, in a way.

B: But why? I can't see this at all, unless you're playing tendentiously with the feminine stereotype.

A: "Why?" may be the wrong question. Maybe the right question is "why not?"

B: Come on: it's too easy to turn things around that way.

A: It's not just a matter of turning things around. It's also possible to give it some justification.

B: Let's hear it.

A: To a large extent, you've already heard it. I tried to explain earlier that the *homo faber*'s characteristic activeness is not an accidental element, but a true necessity for the carrier of the realist paradigm. And note: a conceptual, not a physical necessity. What men and women do, the movements performed by their bodies, will remain exactly the same, but the realist must *conceive* at least some of these movements as the result of an activity, *and hence* of a free choice on the subject's part. Otherwise there is no hope for him of understanding anything, or of understanding himself. But we can't say that this continuous reference to an action and a choice is conceptually satisfactory. In a sense, it only consecrates our lack of understanding, since a choice is precisely the point where all explanation ends, or if you will the story begins.

B: You don't seem to have a very positive idea of human freedom.

A: That's right, but the problem is too large for us to face now. Let's limit ourselves to saying that it's conceptually awkward and embarrassing to think and talk about action: for whenever this term is used a new element of arbitrariness is introduced, a new "beginning." So if we can do without this reference to action, if we can understand—or better, explain what it means "to understand"—in a different way, then it seems natural to drop this awkward, cumbersome pachyderm.

B: With a big noise, it seems. You want a revision of the whole concept of understanding, nothing less.

A: And you find it strange? We're talking about universal, galactic turnabouts of thought, and you believe that such a central notion as understanding can go unscathed?

B: No, for sure. How could I possibly believe that? So tell me now of Achilles, son of Peleus—or rather, I'm sorry, of this new galactic turnabout.

A: I realize we're all a bit tired. I'll try to be brief.

B: I've heard that one before.

A: No, look, in this case it's true, since I can refer to classical models. Before people got intoxicated with the new science and the myth of the lab, the idea of understanding I have in mind was in fact the most common one. Aristotle, for example, was an extremely subtle and perceptive observer, but in his scientific practice we find very little that could be called an experiment in the modern sense of the term. For good reason: if experiments modify the environment then they might modify what we were trying to understand, too, and thus make us understand something else. In order really to understand, we must let the environment speak to us, and hence become receptive toward it, and hence again get ourselves integrated into it: not violate it to prove our power—or better, our stupid, childish power mania—but rather subject ourselves to it, as to something infinitely more vast, powerful, and lasting than us, whose laws we'll capture only by assimilating ourselves to them, by making them *our own*, by letting ourselves be absorbed, as a live, conscious, but also respectful presence within the great flux of being.

A: Yours is quite a strange Aristotle: a bit mystical and a bit feminist.

B: As usual, it all depends on the frame of reference. I don't believe that Aristotle was especially mystical or feminist; indeed I believe that he made a lot of progress—with all the ambiguity surrounding spatial qualifications of this kind—in clarifying the mode of thinking I called "male." His idea that objects—or substances, or *ousiai*—should be defined as what exists in a primary sense, *and nothing else*, that is, that there should be no need, or possibility, of a deeper determination of the *notion* of an object, fits perfectly with the priority that the male paradigm assigns to this notion. Still, Aristotle comes before Galileo, that is, before those technological developments which confer on this paradigm not so much greater theoretical dignity as more concrete effectiveness. Thus, when facing the everyday reality of contact with the world, and the persistent problem of establishing a fruitful relation of coexistence with it, he's almost insensibly led to fall back onto what worked so far: a resonance, an attention, an accord that don't quite fit his fundamental theses but still haven't found credible alternatives.

B: So, an Aristotle not so much feminist as indecisive, who while trying to develop new ideas is still stuck with the old practices.

A: That's one way to put it.

B: And a history that goes from female to male: from a model of integration, respect, and maybe even passivity, to one that privileges instead imposition, domination, and violence.

A: This I find doubtful. Not because I believe that things went differently, but because it doesn't seem to me that the way they went should be extrapolated to a general pattern of history, a one-directional plan finding its implacable realization within a time just as unitary. No, time for me is an arena for uncertain, entangled wanderings, and history doesn't exist. There are *stories* instead, the thousand bizarre episodes of a forced coexistence among diverse, inimical realities; the unpredictable courses, the tortuous meanders of a flux whose only law is that of least resistance. Looking back from where we are, we try to weave together these accidental, confused events, and maybe if we spend enough time and energy in it we'll succeed, for the brief stretch that we can travel with our own, and other people's, memory—except for being surprised by the next turn of what our powerlessness and desperation force us to call destiny.

B: Sounds like poetry, but what does it tell us?

A: It tells us that the path from Aristotle to Kant—and possibly the longer path that begins even further back, in some Mediterranean culture of a matriarchal or matrilineal character—is nothing but an episode: maybe a pendulum swing of unknown period, or just a Brownian movement of excited, puzzled particles. History doesn't go from female to male—not because it goes in a different direction, but because it goes in *no* particular direction at all. The very notion of direction is foreign to it: it's an invention of ours. *We* can't live without a direction; history and the world can perfectly well do without one.

B: Still you claim that we must intervene in this history, do our best to change it, make the two paradigms interact.

A: What I claim is that part of our being in the world consists in making projects, in telling ourselves how the world has bent before our will or rebelled against it, and how the one and the other have been natural consequences of the justice or the error in which we're immersed, of the merits we've acquired, of the sins we're paying for. I claim that our most frequently recurring temptation is that of making ourselves responsible for the world and interpreting its behavior as a function of our moves, as a response to them, as a prize or a punishment for them.

B: Where the whole thing is merely a gigantic daydream?

A: I don't know that much, since I'm myself embedded in this reality, and I can only see my living in the world in terms of a project. It's in these terms, then, that one must understand what I said. Men—males, to be clearer—wanted to conquer and dominate the world, and wagered that domination would bring them salvation and prosperity. For this purpose, they conceived and treated the environment as their own creation, as a toy: their nursery, or more respectfully their lab, extended all the way to the last horizon, and their ideal was that of manipulating things, of changing them. In the short term this ideal was a winning one, but we're already seeing signs that it's getting stuck, we're already noticing its wrinkles, we're beginning to understand that it was a simplistic, reductive, childish project. We played with fire and we're getting burned. With one last leap of pride, using the inertial speed already acquired, the model tries to survive by silencing all alternative voices, drowning them in its arrogant noise and ostentatious confidence. The reason is obvious: if nothing else is available, we'll have to rest content with this brutal, truculent logic, indeed we'll consider it the only one possible.

B: Which it is not.

A: No, but for it not to be so someone must take up the burden of the *other* possibilities, must extend the spectrum of alternatives, defend and use them so as to make them credible and practical. And this is, I believe, the historical task of the feminine element . . .

B: That is, the task of a dialectical integration . . .

A: Exactly: of a structural enrichment, of a search, of an excavation . . .

C: You're despicable.

B: Despicable? What do you mean?

A: It's natural for her to talk like that, Bertoldo. The conditioning of the feminine element was as subtle as it was effective. Deviant moves were silenced by incorporating them: women were promised the same doubtful salvation as men if they agreed to become like men. No wonder, then, if in this situation it's so difficult for them to acquire consciousness of their "novelty."

C: Yes, despicable, and maddening, too.

B: Why maddening? It doesn't seem that we're expressing anti-feminist views. Indeed, as far as I'm concerned . . .

C: Yes, I know. You could defend the feminine element better than it defends itself. And the same is true for your friend. And you don't notice, either of you, the stench exhaling from your position.

B: "Stench" sounds a bit strong.

C: It is, but one needs strong words to express strong feelings. See, I've been sitting here for a couple of hours, listening to you, saying nothing, and you know why? Do you know what I invested all this time in?

B: In your glass, I imagine, if our words are so rotten and senseless.

C: Now you return to a level more appropriate to a woman: your expressions are lighter and funnier. You spoke like this at the beginning, remember, and to explain why you both chattered about an embarrassment toward me, a lack of "historical" preparation, gaps in the conceptual scheme. Whereas the matter is much simpler: to a woman, with a woman, one never speaks in a serious way. One laughs at her, as you do, or one delivers a sermon to her, as he does. As soon as I shut up, your tone changed, the embarrassment vanished, my presence was no longer felt.

B: We got carried away with excitement . . .

C: Who are you trying to kid, Bertoldo? It was instructive to listen to you both, and compare *what* you said with *how* you said it. You spoke about women—you, Angelo, told a story about women who should become protagonists, subjects of important conceptual and technological revolutions . . .

A: Conceptual, primarily.

C: Sure, sure, tell me all the details. And while you raised the issue of how women could best get to owning their destiny and offering mankind a larger spectrum of options, of this woman before you, who was listening to you, you didn't even feel like asking a question.

B: But there was no need to ask you anything: we could all speak whenever we wanted.

A: That's right, and I also think that asking you would have reinforced the parochial prejudice: only women should speak about women, and maybe about nothing else.

C: So many protestations! The truth is that you were perfectly happy to speak to one another, and showed no desire for an external intervention, let alone a woman's.

A: But it's precisely this intervention that I said is necessary!

C: No, Angelo. What you said had its own precise logic. It originated in a problem created by men for men, and called women in question only as saviors—that is, once more, as functional to someone else's design, to a goal that is not theirs.

A: Why? Are they not part of mankind? Will they not be saved or lost with the rest of us?

C: Sure, but they'll be saved or lost on *their* conditions, following *their* plans, and possibly making *their* mistakes. You insisted so much on violence at the beginning, but seem not to realize how much violence and exploitation there is under the conciliatory and peaceful appearance of your proposal. So far, you say, men got everything wrong: they conceived the world as a projection of theirs, or as a toy, and in this way they corrupted, polluted, and almost destroyed it. Women are among the many things they corrupted: they were conditioned to play the same role as men and forced by objective limitations to play it badly. So what's needed is for women to fix everything: to get into what you called the nursery and tidy it up. What's needed is for them to put out the fire, to be your mommies again. You scream, "What a mess! What did we get ourselves into! Help, help!" and we run and save you from the consequences of your irresponsible behavior.

A: Why? How would you solve the problem?

C: I don't know, and I don't *have to* know. Becoming protagonists of history means just this: that one need not account for one's behavior to others, one need not follow and serve goals and tasks dictated by others. It means situating oneself in history, having the courage to occupy space and not feel forced to justify this space, to give an excuse for keeping it.

A: A purely voluntarist position, in other words.

C: Maybe, but didn't you say that stories and projects are just *a posteriori* rationalizations of moves already made, of practices that will forever continue blindly on their way—whatever the rationalization? Well, so far the practice was that man was at the center of attention and woman turned around him: an obscure, humble satellite with no light of its own. *This practice* doesn't change in the story you tell: it's only that the satellite proves a little more useful than one thought. And, most important, the same practice remains unchanged in your behavior, in your carrying on a dialogue at a high intellectual level with your male friend while according a woman only inspired prophecies and cheap jokes, in your *saying* that you want so much to know my opinion while never in fact showing any real curiosity, any real interest.

A: But I told you: I act like this because I'm myself conditioned, I'm myself an expression of the culture I criticize.

C: Well, then, if you're an expression of this despicable culture, get out of the way. Don't tell us what to do, don't try to extend your dead hand over our liberation. We don't know yet what to do, we haven't had time to think about it, we've spent all our time listening to the ramblings of individuals like yourself. Make room, leave us alone, we don't need any burdensome bequests or thankless tasks: you guys had none when you started. We want the right to look for ourselves, to wander as you did until we have found our story, which is not and cannot be the one *you* told because *our* identity is what's in question and *we* must decide on it. I'm not sure that the crumbs you've left us will be enough, you may have ruined everything beyond any possibility of redemption, we may have lost before we even had a chance to play, but, for God's sake, enough of your chatter.

Carletto

CARLETTO: Hi guys, what are you doing here? I would never have thought of finding you lost in contemplation of this fresco, in a place so out of the way.

ANGELO: To tell you the truth, it's much stranger to see you in this place, Carletto, considering how involved you always are in "things that matter."

C: Things matter because there are people who make them matter, Angelo. People who decide to make them matter long before anyone else thinks of it, and who move and prepare everything without anyone noticing.

BERTOLDO: Are you saying that something is cooking here?

C: I'm not saying it's not.

B: Couldn't you be more precise?

C: I don't know. Certainly I wouldn't want to see my plans spread all over tomorrow's papers.

B: Come on, Carletto, you don't think that we have such privileged access to the media.

A: Sure he does. He has it, and so do all the people he associates with—or he wouldn't associate with them. So how could he imagine that someone is cut off from those channels?

C: Here goes the pure intellectual, always ready to attack those trying to get culture out of its ivory tower and closer to the public—which after all pays for intellectuals and their towers.

A: "Public" is a nice word that solves many problems. Unfortunately, like many similar panaceas, it solves them by playing on an ambiguity.

C: What ambiguity? Don't get too fancy. Some things are public and some private, and that's all. For example, there is you entertaining yourself and there is me trying to establish a dialogue with people.

A: Don't get upset, Carletto; I'm not being fancy. The problem is simply this: what people shall we establish a dialogue with? The ancient Romans' "public thing" concerned only a few, just like the "democracy" of Greek cities. All these words contain a hidden parameter, an implicit free variable, and as long as the variable is not interpreted, the parameter is not given a value, their use is confused and demagogic. On the other hand, clarifying one's intentions might make one's position much less attractive: for example, if we specified that by "public opinion"—that is, common opinion—we mean the one that is common to the readers of certain magazines, the visitors to certain exhibitions, the guests at certain parties, we could hardly be mistaken for those progressive intellectuals we want to be mistaken for. So it's best to keep things vague: what the eye doesn't see (or, in this case, the ear doesn't hear) . . .

C: All right, you reinvented the wheel. Acting in the real world requires compromises, and getting bound to structures that make it possible for you to act. Do you have any alternative in mind?

A: No, but I don't think I have to propose an alternative before I point out the problems with other positions.

C: But that's too easy! If you can't think of the right way, or at least a better way, of doing things, it's meaningless for you to call others wrong.

A: Maybe, but then I'm not a threat and there's no need to get so excited.

B: If I can interrupt for a second, there would seem to be an obvious alternative. One could extend the scope of "public" to all society—if you will, bind the free variable with a universal quantifier. In particular, one could have art shared by everyone, not just the members of certain circles.

C: Yes, great. You think it's a critic's job to change society? And, even if it were, what is the critic *as a critic* supposed to do until society changes? Get another job, let himself be stalled, write works no one reads? As things are, most people have no access to what I care about, and even if they did they wouldn't know what to do with it, because society is what it is and forces them to worry about other things, for example surviving.

I know all this, yet I'm not ready to give up my profession, for it is what I do best. So I do it as I can, with whoever I can.

A: Like the art-world phonies you hang out with?

C: Why not? Do you think I'm ashamed to be seen with them?

A: I'm sure you're not. I probably would be.

B: Look, both of you, let's try to raise the level of the conversation. That was below the belt, Angelo: personal attacks are not allowed.

A: I don't know that it was only a personal attack: I was talking about a whole form of life. But I agree that the remark was unfair, and I apologize.

C: All right, but to move on to something more constructive than an apology you might explain to me what you guys are doing here, in front of Piero's *Resurrection*. Since you don't want to discuss "political" alternatives, let's talk about personal choices, and perhaps from these we might extract a meaning that goes beyond the single individual—without specifying at the moment how far.

A: I believe the meaning you're looking for will be easy to extract. Indeed, it might be possible to extract several, one for each ideological position. As far as I'm concerned, I must say that my most important reason for coming here was the fascination of a pilgrimage

C: This is really something! Have you taken a turn toward the spiritual?

A: Far from it. The world we live in—that indeed seems to me a very "spiritual" reality, in the sense that it's abstract, disconnected from the concrete, solid, physical support of matter, lost in the creation, and even more the *re*creation, the reproduction, of certain images and schemes.

C: Try to get concrete yourself, or you're going to lose me.

A: Think of all you have, everything that belongs to you, and even what doesn't belong to you but is all around you, occupying your life, functioning as your environment and possibly as your interlocutor. Think of your house, your car, your furniture, your clothes, your watch. Think of your books, your newspapers, your records. Each of these things comes in indefinitely many copies, all virtually interchangeable. Which means that none of these things is important because of its individuality, but only because it embodies a model, an idea. And also that, in a world so deprived of individuality, even your own person runs serious risks. You, too, might perhaps be scattered in tens of copies, and this particular one you care so much about might be no more important than any other.

C: Wait a minute, you're going too fast. Even admitting, for the sake of argument, that this reproducibility extends to all the *individual* objects in our world, it doesn't follow that our personality is affected by it. We

Piero della Francesca. *The Resurrection of Christ.* Pinacoteca
Comunale, Sansepolcro, Italy. (Alinari/Art Resource, NY).

need only move to a different level: instead of finding what makes us
"unique" in some unrepeatable object, we'll find it in an unrepeatable
combination of objects, all themselves repeatable. The way we *structure*
objects around us—not the brute, obtuse reality of a piece of matter—will
provide us with a possibility of identification.

A: Maybe. But I'm beginning to miss this brute, obtuse reality. I feel a sort of subtle regret for an object that doesn't require efforts of projection and placement on my part, that presents itself as already identified, as *that one* and no other. A painful, possibly morbid desire for an object like this to tell me what I am, not vice versa. That's why I set out for *this* city, *this* building, *this* room, because only *here*, here *and nowhere else*, there is, *there can be, this* object.

C: All this is quite touching, but also a bit gratuitous. For the possibility of reproduction you were mentioning is not limited to new things. In principle, what would prevent some sophisticated technology from reproducing this painting with total exactness? I mean all the brushstrokes constituting it, with all their chemical structure, maybe even in the same order they were originally laid down?

A: Nothing would prevent it, you're right. Still, the result wouldn't be the same object, it would only be a copy of it, in a different sense of the word "copy" from the one used before: the *a*symmetrical sense in which one makes copies *of an original*, which remains *the only* original.

C: You'll have to get clearer on this.

A: I'll try. The thousands of cars, TV sets, microwaves coming out of a factory are not just identical to one another: they also lack all history. They're born together from a design that exists on paper or in some other hardware: a design that in any case is *not* itself a car or a TV set or a microwave. So it's natural to consider them inessential instantiations of an abstract model, insignificant material appendices to the only thing that really matters: the design, the idea. With the *Resurrection* it's a different story. In this case the object has already existed for five hundred years, and nothing can change that: it's a logical law, of the logic of our time and our experience, that what has already happened will never change, will remain true whatever the future course of the world might be. Nothing can change the fact that for five hundred years men and women from the whole world have stood in veneration, or in anger, or with indifference, in front of *this* painting, and that for five hundred years *there wasn't* the sort of exact copy you were talking about. For five hundred years this painting was the only example of itself: an exact copy produced now would only be a pale imitation of it, for a copy could only reproduce its surface, its external image, but not the history permeating it—a history that step by step has changed it, and is no longer available to change *anything else*, not *in the same way*.

C: But then you agree with me. Aren't you moving from the level of a purely physical, material reality to one where what counts is the relations between physical, material entities—in this case between the painting and the men and women who stood in front of it?

A: Yes, in a way, but I would want you to reflect on how different this case is from the one you seemed to have in mind earlier. When you spoke of an "unrepeatable combination of objects, all themselves repeatable," the picture I got, perhaps because I know you, is that of a famous architect or interior designer putting together a precious eighteenth-century cupboard, a science-fiction-like lamp, and who knows what other devilish tricks, to create an "absolutely personal" environment for the VIP who hired him. There is something ephemeral, evanescent in such an assemblage. It's a pure and simple aggregate of different elements, which *we* created—and which we might at any moment, and just as playfully, replace with another.

C: Whereas you have in mind something much more serious, it seems.

A: I'm not sure whether "serious" is the right word. I keep coming up with words like "solid," "physical," "concrete." And I realize that it's strange, for what I find solid and concrete, here, is some kind of precipitate of the feelings, the passions, the joy and sorrow of those who were actors in or spectators of an event or an object. It's strange because feelings and passions seem paradigmatic examples of things *without* solidity and concreteness; still, when they were lively and deep, you can sense them echoing in the air, and conferring on this air a strange thickness, an intensity that can even hurt. I remember my visit to Mauthausen, the long time I spent in the shower room: there were screams and cries all around me, presences that wouldn't have impressed a photographic plate but still forced themselves on my attention more than any other, more than I could stand.

C: With all due respect for your feelings, we've gotten quite far from what is normally understood as "concrete."

A: So what? "Normally," as you say, we're interested in concrete things because they know how to get themselves noticed. If you behave as if the wall weren't there, you might run into it and get hurt, so it's best to pay it due attention. Turning the tables—or, in more dignified terms, inverting the order of conceptual dependence—one might characterize concreteness itself as the property that something has when it imposes itself on us, when it demands respect, when we can't help acknowledging it, on pain of getting hurt.

C: So your atavistic regret for something physical and concrete becomes the regret for something that imposes itself on you, that it's necessary for you to come to terms with.

A: I'd say yes. And I'd also say that this is what my desire for identification, for uniqueness, reduces to. The best evidence that something exists, people have always said, is that it acts; the best evidence that it's distinct from everything else—we might add—is that its action is distinct from that of everything else. What forces itself on us, what demands respect, what causes emotion and pain, undeniably *is*, and is *what it is* and nothing else if the emotion it causes is distinct from any other.

C: I believe I understand. But there remains the problem of why, in this search for genuine, unrepeatable sensations, you came here. Why didn't you go to another concentration camp? Why didn't you climb Mount Everest?

B: Maybe it's my turn to answer here. The fact is that around this trip, this "pilgrimage" as Angelo called it, gathered a number of different needs—and perhaps if they hadn't we wouldn't have come, for it's one thing to talk about traveling to Sansepolcro and quite another to get on the road and do it.

C: Especially with the traffic these days.

B: That's right, though I must say that once one gets here, away from all the official routes, one has the unexpected reward of an almost unreal calm, of a silence and solitude, at this time of day, that are themselves worth the whole trip.

C: Wait until we have redesigned the "official routes," and then you'll see.

B: I'm not sure I want to see. But to return to our motivations—or more precisely to mine—I was hoping this trip might help me solve a big problem: that of having no artistic sense. Faced with a painting, a sculpture, a play, or a movie, I see people utter, with absolute confidence, lavish praises or irrevocable condemnations, and others seem to understand: they agree, or maybe disagree on some details, but they always remain on the same wavelength, as it were. Some of these people are clearly experts, from whom one might expect a firm judgment, but others . . .

C: . . . are only hypocrites, who hide under their arrogance a total lack of preparation, and who bank on everyone else's insecurity and on the elusive nature of these themes to establish a reputation for artistic sensitivity.

B: Maybe. But I keep wondering whether the hypocrites aren't just a part of this crowd, perhaps even the majority, but not all of it, or at least not *necessarily* all of it, and hence whether I lack something that it's at least *possible* to have.

C: This existential anxiety seems unjustified. Do you have any reason to think that you lack something?

B: Not an empirical reason, for, as you suggested, in these cases it's difficult to distinguish the real thing from a fake, the presence of an authentic meaning from a complacent wordiness or, even worse, from the attempt to acquire an undeserved prestige. But there's a general reason—an *a priori* one, to use an old-fashioned phrase—that maintains a remarkable influence on me, and I'm not ready to give it up without convincing evidence.

C: This *a priori* of yours sounds a lot like a prejudice.

B: Maybe, but—to put it *à la* Gadamer—our prejudices are also our inevitable starting points, and doing without them only means refusing to get involved in that risky but also exhilarating adventure that the human condition is.

C: You're really evolving, Bertoldo. A while ago you wouldn't have cited Gadamer. Whatever happened to the Carnaps and the Poppers? Are they no longer the fad?

A: You're doing him an injustice, Carletto: fads don't matter. Bertoldo is one of the few people I know who can still learn something.

C: Especially when you teach him, so you're both happy.

B: Let's stop this squabble and return to my *a priori* motivation. I believe that art—Art with a capital A, I mean . . .

C: I'm not at all sure what you mean. What is to be included, and—even more important—excluded, by this qualification?

B: I don't know. I'm confused, and I was trying to resolve the confusion. Maybe all I mean is that something is really art and something else only passes as art, but it's not.

C: Well, if that's all . . .

B: Look, I'm not trying to be original; in this field I'd be happy to just understand something. Specifically, I'd like to understand how far I should trust a principle I've always agreed with in the abstract but have serious problems with *in concreto*: the principle according to which true art should communicate its meaning, its value, and possibly a certain amount of "aesthetic pleasure" to everyone, without discrimination, whatever their level of cultural formation and sophistication, their "preparation" as you called it. If this principle is true, then I face the following dilemma: either I've never encountered true art, or I'm in such a subhuman state that what communicates to everyone, what everyone seems to be able to pass deep, self-conscious judgments on, tells me nothing at all.

C: I insist that your anxiety is uncalled for. As I see it, you have a real problem, which should be addressed with the proper tools and all the necessary attention and patience, without hoping for instantaneous, miraculous remedies, and you also have a fictitious problem, which troubles you and prevents you from facing the *other* problem with due care—much like the person who, finding himself in a sudden danger, must fight not only the danger itself but also the panic that overwhelms him and makes it difficult for him to act safely and effectively.

B: Try to be clearer. Images are O.K., but literal statements are even better.

C: All right. Your real problem is that you don't have enough artistic education. It's not your fault, but rather the fault of an educational system that privileges science and literature while paying little attention to plastic and figurative arts, let alone music. So, when you find yourself in front of a painting, you don't know what to say, because first you don't have the proper vocabulary, and then even if you did have it you wouldn't know how to use it, that is, wouldn't know what to look for and how to apply the technical terms to what you see. After reading many sonnets and many novels at school, guided by someone who knows how to read them, you're perfectly able to decide on your own whether a sonnet is original or derivative, nostalgic or vigorous, and whether a novel is terse or wordy, well-constructed or inconclusive. But, since you didn't do this kind of exercise with paintings, when you're faced with a painting—even admitting that you overheard expressions like "plastic sense," "luminosity," or "compositional structure"—you're too embarrassed to use them, and if you still try to do so, like the arrogant chatterers we were talking about, the result is pure word-salad.

B: Whereas the solution would be . . .

C: Until things change radically—and, as I told Angelo earlier, we certainly can't sit around waiting until then—the solution must be found in the social role of the critic, who, after filling the gaps in his education with personal effort and discipline and maybe even by the sheer luck of belonging to a certain "environment," proposes himself as a guide for a long, tiresome journey of recovery of these latent, mortified potentialities.

B: So you're saying that society should go back to school, and the critic should be its teacher?

C: Yes, as the only valid alternative—in the present state of affairs—to the aphasia of honest people like you, on the one hand, and the meaning-

Piero della Francesca. *Flagellation.* Galleria Nazionale, Urbino, Italy.
(Alinari/Art Resource, NY).

less noise of those less than honest, on the other. And take my word that
after some good schooling you would no longer be embarrassed in front
of a painting: you would be able to use the right words and, what counts
most, *explain them* on request. It would no longer be a matter of scattering
words at random, but of understanding what one says. And understanding
would be accompanied by pleasure: the pleasure of recognizing the meaning of what one sees, of following the technical difficulties faced by the
expression of that meaning, and of grasping the ingenuity (if any) of the
solutions to them.

B: Could you give an example?

C: Well, since I found you in front of a Piero della Francesca, I'll cite
a fitting case. Take the *Flagellation*, in Urbino. What Piero means by this
painting is: you're constantly spectators of a violence that repeats to
infinity the old blasphemous insult to Christ. In order to "say" all this with
a painting, one must face and solve two problems. First, the painting—in
contrast, say, with a symphony or a tragedy—has no temporal dimension,
and hence can't represent directly the *before* and *after* that make sense of

the idea of repetition. Second, the meaning involves something, indeed someone, who literally is not and cannot be part of the figurative content—the viewer. The first problem is solved by dividing the painting in two parts, one smaller than the other to suggest a temporal distinction. In Piero's time, one received an additional clue to this meaning from the figures in the foreground, whom one was probably able to recognize as contemporary characters (hence as characters *not* contemporary with Christ), but this clue is redundant: even without knowing that the blond youth is (say) Oddantonio da Montefeltro, we can reconstruct the temporality of the message by examining the compositional structure of the work (and here is one of the expressions I mentioned earlier, used in a perfectly appropriate way). The second problem is more subtle, and so is its solution. By comparing the two scenes, the one closer and the one farther away, one notices a symmetry: there are two groups of three people, where the person in the middle seems to be a "victim" of the other two. But the symmetry is broken by the fact that, in the scene farther away, there are also two additional people. So it becomes natural for the viewer *to look for* the two missing people in the scene closer up, and (if he has the time and the patience) finally to recognize one of them—the one with his back to us, who not accidentally appears almost in relief, almost external to the painting's surface—in . . . himself, who indeed, being outside the painting, cannot be represented in it. Once this is understood, the message comes through clearly: what you're looking at is the same scene of violence that was performed once before and will probably return, implacably, as long as humanity survives.

B: And the other additional person?

C: He reinforces the ineluctable character of this message. He is another spectator—a strange one, with a funny hat, like someone from a faraway land who is not too worried about what he sees, but rather detached and indifferent. He's an image of chance, or if you will of destiny, the omnipotent and absent-minded artificer of human events—of these tiresomely, brutally, pointlessly repetitive events. And there isn't a corresponding character in the foreground because chance continues to dominate us, well beyond the "historical" scenes reproduced by Piero.

B: It's a brilliant example, which clarifies very well how the time and effort spent in interpreting a work, and in providing oneself with the tools needed to carry out such interpretations, can be rewarded by the intimate pleasure of establishing a dialogue with the artist, of understanding his most secret intentions. But I'm left with a doubt . . .

C: Just a moment. Before we get to doubts, let me finish. I told you that you have two problems, one real and one fictitious. So far I've discussed the first; now we need to briefly address the second.

B: Yes. What's this impediment that troubles me and prevents me from seriously engaging in my artistic education?

C: It's the pseudoromantic illusion of an "easy" art, close to everyone's feelings and experiences, naturally comprehensible, devoid of technique. I sometimes suspect that this ideology was coined on purpose, to cover up the pedagogic disaster I mentioned earlier and throw the responsibility for it on the individual. "It's your fault if you don't understand," he's told in essence, "since art is made to be understood without mediation by all human beings, or at least all normal human beings, among whom you clearly don't belong." And it matters little that almost no one belongs among them: this concept of normality is not statistical but, again, ideological, so its point is to hide real difficulties behind self-serving images.

B: I understand, and I agree. Up to a point, at least, for I'm still bothered by my doubt.

C: Go ahead, then: it's time to discuss it.

B: The problem is this. Earlier, when I was rambling about Art with a capital A, I spoke in a confused, entangled way of three aspects that seem to be present in any aesthetic phenomenon. I spoke of the *meaning* of this phenomenon, of its *value*, and of a certain *pleasure* that accompanies its appreciation. Of course, I wouldn't have known how to relate these three aspects; if I spoke of them it's only because I had in turn heard of them. Now from what you say there emerges a precise proposal about this relation, which in my own words I would express more or less as follows. The *meaning* of a work of art is what the artist wants to communicate to his public through the work, by using a specific language. Since every language has its limitations and its problems of expression, there will be obstacles to communicating certain contents: a work's *value* is to be found in the ingenuity, the originality, and perhaps the economy of the solutions the artist finds to overcome these obstacles. Which entails, among other things, and in agreement with common sense, that the communication of trivial contents has little artistic value. Finally, an adequate appreciation of the work requires a precise commitment on the part of the public to understand the problems faced by the artist and his solutions of them, and the *pleasure* caused by this appreciation will be greater, the higher the level of understanding reached.

C: Perfect! You really have a splendid capacity for synthesis. And now tell me where things don't add up for you.

B: At the last step, when aesthetic pleasure comes in. For you, if

I'm following what you say, this pleasure is a concomitant effect of the operation of recognizing a meaning, and must increase as the work is understood *better*.

C: You followed very well.

B: But then explain to me why the things we understand the best—say, the weather forecast or the news—those we can recognize and control with absolute confidence, *give us no pleasure*—not necessarily, at least. Is it a pseudoromantic delusion that the appreciation of a work of art calls us in question, forces us to risk something, and that even when it seems to give way to understanding and calm it still hides, at least potentially, a further mystery, an enigma that is not yet understood and may never be? You, too, spoke of labor, of tension, of effort. What's the relation between this labor and pleasure? Is labor needed for there to be pleasure? Why?

C: Because there is not always something to understand, and when there is then some effort—however minimal—is needed. What is there to understand in a chair you sit on every day? Nothing: the chair sends no message. There is, behind the chair, no will to establish a relation, to communicate with you. But now an artist takes a chair and puts it in a museum, not so that people can sit on it to admire the works of art, but as a work of art itself. In this case, the artist is using the chair to tell you something, there is indeed something to understand, and in order to understand it you must learn to look at things from a viewpoint which is not your own, must ask yourself: "What is this guy trying to tell me? What's his language, his frame of reference? Why does he express himself in this way?"

B: O.K., but notice how different our examples are. You speak of a chair on which I sit every day and, since you seem to have an "intentionalist" view of meaning—the meaning of an action must be found in the agent's intentions—it's easy for you to deny that in this case there's any meaning to be understood. Whereas I spoke of the weather forecast, that is, of something that exists because of a speaker's action *and of his intention to communicate with us*. But, *contra* your proposal, even if we understand this speaker's message perfectly well, such a "recognition" is accompanied by no pleasure.

C: Look, I'm convinced that in the everyday world—the world of weather forecasts and shopping lists—there's absolutely nothing to understand. Everything happens automatically, blindly, with the logic of a conditioned reflex. I don't see any sign there of that specifically intellectual activity which I would call understanding.

B: Maybe, but now your position risks becoming empty. As long as you use the word "understanding" in an ordinary way, as more or less everyone else uses it, that is, in such a way that it can be applied to both the news and an opera or an avant-garde play, your thesis that aesthetic pleasure results from understanding a message has a precise content, perhaps questionable but nonetheless substantial. But if, when faced by examples where one understands—or at least *believes* one understands—something without however feeling any pleasure, you assert that the examples are not genuine, that *really*, contrary to what one thinks, there is nothing in them to be understood, the suspicion naturally arises that your thesis reduces to a tautology, a triviality: aesthetic pleasure results from understanding a message; but understanding is so defined that if there is no pleasure there is no understanding, either.

A: This conclusion seems too radical, Bertoldo. Carletto did something more than define the question so that things come out right for him: not much more perhaps, but enough to grant him the benefit of the doubt.

C: Yes, Angelo, give me a hand. With you professional philosophers, I always end up feeling cornered.

B: I'm not sure you'll like the hand he gives you. He has a way of turning people's positions upside down . . .

C: I know, but after all it's a harmless game. And one that might give me some ideas.

A: Let's hope so. Carletto has indeed given a sketch of a reason for why "in the everyday world there's nothing to understand." He said that in this world "everything happens automatically," and insists that just this "automatism" is incompatible with the "intellectual" phenomenon of understanding. By developing these suggestions I think we could go well beyond the trivialities Bertoldo is so worried about.

B: I'd like to know how.

A: The most promising starting point is perhaps to be found in what we could call "philosophical grammar." The problem, that is, is deciding what sort of thing understanding is, to what "category" it belongs. It seems that on this point there is an irreconcilable difference between Carletto and you—which constitutes the foundation of all your disagreements.

C: See what I mean? Your language always has such a sublime abstractness, such an elegance . . .

A: Never mind the compliments; I know all too well that they're a double-edged sword. Abstractness implies lack of realism, childishness. And in some sense I think you're right, but let everyone do his job.

B: Yes, let's get to the point. What categorial difference do you have in mind?

A: I believe it's best to begin by analyzing the notion of understanding certain modes of expression, a certain language; later, it shouldn't be too difficult to extend what I say to the understanding of specific "episodes," of particular expressions formulated *in* that language. With this qualification, it seems that for you, Bertoldo, understanding is a *state*, just as, for example, it's a state to be seated or to be President of the U.S. One *sits down*, or *becomes* (is elected) President, and from then on *remains in the state* of being seated, or of being President, until something happens to deprive him of that state (say, he gets up, or his term expires). *If nothing happens* (or better, nothing relevant, since the earth may well continue to turn, and so on), his state of being seated or being President won't change, either. In the same way, you think that, at a certain time, after a number of experiences and after traveling a certain existential path, one gets to the point of understanding, say, the news or the weather forecast, and from then on continues to understand them, *unless something happens*, for example he's hit by a rock or collapses into schizophrenia.

B: Your reconstruction is fair. And now I'm curious to hear how else it's possible to account for this notion.

A: Always the same story! Our ideas aren't just ours, they're the only possible ones. Which, incidentally, I think, makes them less valuable, for it turns them into what everyone should believe if only they had enough common sense. Whereas it's precisely *against* common sense that we must go, other people's *and our own*, forever asking under what conditions what seems natural to us could be *false*.

B: Don't change the subject. Such declarations of principle won't help you: I want a specific answer.

A: The answer is not difficult. Carletto—or maybe I should say a sympathetic rational reconstruction of Carletto, call him Carletto*—takes understanding to be an *action*, something done, and hence something that goes out of existence the moment it's no longer being done. Consider the case of the chair presented in a museum as a work of art. The visitor enters the museum, sees the chair, realizes on the basis of some environmental details that it doesn't have its usual function but is rather to be understood as a "work of art"—for example, no one sits on it, the chair is cordoned off, there's a title by it—and raises, more or less consciously, the problem of decoding the message the artist wants to communicate, and of mastering the language in which he wants to communicate it. He thus begins an activity of interpretation, calling on all his patience and inventiveness (just as the artist originally did), and at the end of this activity he might conclude that the message is as follows: "Whatever is placed in an institutionalized context like this museum will be considered a work of art, so art is primarily a social phenomenon." Now the key phrase here is "at the end": the result thus obtained *closes* the operation of understanding. *After* reaching this result—and assuming that it is correct and exhaustive—there's nothing more to understand, *and nothing more gets understood*, since understanding was precisely the interpretive activity I described, an activity that now *is over*.

B: And what would Carletto* call the state that follows the completion of this activity? Wouldn't he call it the state of one who *understands* the meaning of the chair?

C: It's nice to be starred like this, and transformed into a purely rational entity, free from one's conditioning, redeemed from one's inessential errors.

A: No, for him that would be the state of one who *has already understood* the meaning of the chair, just as the state of one who has finished climbing a mountain is that of one who has already climbed. Whoever has already climbed is no longer climbing, and whoever has already understood is no longer understanding—though both may profit from what they did. The one who has climbed can take beautiful pictures, and the one who has understood can give learned lectures.

B: Yes, but saying that one who has already understood is no longer understanding goes against common sense.

A: Here you go again with common sense. As if common sense were a unitary, integrated structure! In fact, the label "common sense" often hides contradictory views, whose mutual incoherence is not appreciated only because, out of laziness or charity, one doesn't analyze them carefully. For example, Carletto's statement that in the everyday world there's nothing to understand is a fairly common one, and if it's true that it agrees with his categorization of understanding then it's also true that it can't agree with yours. Within common sense one finds everything and its opposite.

C: Thank you for leaving the star out.

A: Besides, even if common sense were coherent, why should *today's* common sense be tomorrow's, too?

C: Sometimes I have the impression that you guys don't even hear others speaking.

A: Let's consider instead the internal structure of this proposal, ask ourselves whether it "holds," and if it does then it might well become tomorrow's common sense—when today's has run its course.

B: You've certainly gone a long way from your defense of empirical realism: now you're showing your true colors.

A: I would prefer other metaphors: say, that of peeling an onion. But, returning to our main theme, one of the results for a person who has already understood is the following: he can use his understanding to react more or less automatically to certain environmental stimuli; for example, to behave appropriately *the next time* he sees a chair in a museum, or, if you will, the next time he watches the news.

B: Wait a minute. It sounds as if you're saying that, when one understands something, this something is always a language, even if it's just an original way of arranging means of expression that are already known. Whatever happened to the episodes you mentioned earlier, and to which you promised you would extend your theory? All I see is a tumult of ever-new languages and a mass of automatic, boring, obtuse replicas of them.

A: Languages are not concrete objects, are not situated in spacetime, and hence it's impossible to assign them precise conditions of identification: to establish for example when we're dealing with *two distinct* languages or with *the same* language to which, say, a single word was added. Such conditions exist only for formal, artificial languages, those we bring to life by an act of will, and which we then give an "ideological" role within the philosophy of language.

B: Now don't change the subject.

A: I mean that it's an entirely arbitrary question whether an artist using certain words or brushstrokes in an original way is inventing a new language or rather using "creatively" what already exists. And, since the question is arbitrary, I'm not interested in it: I have no opinion about it. What interests me—or, if you will, interests the position I'm defending —is that something occurs for which it's legitimate to use the term "understanding" *to the extent that* the artist expresses himself in an original way, and in a way that invites commitment on our part: an originality and a commitment that ordinarily are not present in weather forecasts and in our reception of them.

B: O.K. And pleasure, then, how does it get in here?

A: To get it in, we must make the same fundamental choice we made earlier with respect to the notion of understanding, since the notion of pleasure is just as ambiguous and elusive, and around it the same intellectual battles have been fought and the same general alternatives expressed.

B: You mean "state" or "action"?

A: Exactly. *One* general conception of pleasure, which we could associate, for example, with the Epicurean and Stoic movements, makes it coincide with the absence of stimuli, or at least painful stimuli: a state that might be difficult to achieve, and probably to maintain, but a state nonetheless, which will remain indefinitely identical with itself if nothing happens—or if one can prevent things from happening.

B: Indeed, we could almost say that, in a condition of *ataraxia* like the one you're describing, time no longer exists.

A: Right! Time is the dimension of stimuli, of irritating elements, of all that repeatedly disturbs our peace, rouses us from our torpor, and forces us to become conscious of the world and of ourselves. Without the obsessive, tedious tolling of these stimuli, time would dissolve into an infinite instant, and our personality would be annihilated in the perhaps sweetish, but for many attractive, dream of a vague "unity with the whole."

B: In sum, a true death instinct . . .

A: Yes, and as for the smaller pleasures, say those of the dinner table or of carnal congress . . .

C: You always have such an unpleasant way of putting things! The word "congress" reminds me of eggheads, and in conjunction with "carnal" sounds a bit disgusting. It makes me think of all these bald heads touching, rubbing against each other . . .

A: . . . these are cases where *ataraxia* is reached only for an instant, and then immediately lost under the pressure of uncontrollable environmental demands.

B: But Carletto* would not like *this* notion of pleasure.

C: Here comes the star again.

A: No, he would need the other one, for which I'll refer to *the* philosopher *par excellence*. According to Aristotle, pleasure supervenes upon an activity when the latter reaches perfection. Playing the flute, for example, is something that can be done better or worse. When one gets to the top, to the highest point, one feels pleasure, more precisely *the specific pleasure* associated with playing the flute. And analogously for any other activity.

B: Including the activity of understanding.

A: Yes. And notice that without activity there is no pleasure. Once one stops playing the flute, however great one's ability or popularity as a musician, the pleasure stops, too, though it will reappear without fail the next time one plays, if and when perfection is reached again. In the same way, the activity of understanding reaches its perfection, culminates as it were, when all the pieces of the jigsaw fit and the pattern emerges in all its richness and complexity. This is the unique instant, when one does the best one can within this activity, and hence also feels the purest pleasure. An instant later the operation is over and the pleasure is gone.

B: So our Carletto* would be an Aristotelian.

C: And what about me, without the star? May I, too, aspire to this royal descent?

A: In general, yes. For a more precise formulation of his point of view, however, one would have to resolve some obscurities present in Aristotle himself.

B: For example?

A: For example, shall we say that pleasure occurs only when the activity reaches perfection, or rather that it *increases as* the activity *approaches* perfection? In the latter case, which I would prefer, one could admit that pleasure is possible for those who don't reach perfection, and even that perfection can't be reached but pleasure can. But these are just details.

B: I agree. There are much more serious things we must discuss before we worry about these qualifications.

A: No doubt about it. But I'd like to know what you mean.

B: I mean primarily that I don't like simply putting the two models side by side. Even admitting that they're both coherent, are there arguments in favor of the one or the other, grounds on which a reasonable person might make a choice, or is it just a matter of taste—and as such entirely arbitrary?

A: This easy assimilation of taste and arbitrariness leaves me puzzled; clearly your conversion to Gadamer is still quite superficial. As far as I'm concerned, however, all I can do is articulate my own taste: explain what *I* find more stimulating and productive in one model than in the other.

B: So be it. I realize that I haven't yet mastered your jargon, but the substance of my question remains the same. So which is the model that satisfies *you* more, and possibly for the same reasons should satisfy me, too?

A: I don't like the idea of a "substance" that remains identical to itself through a series of different "manifestations." I'd rather insist on the difference. Also, to be precise, I didn't speak of "satisfying," but of being "stimulating" and "productive."

B: Now don't be pedantic.

A: I'm not. "Satisfying" gives an idea of closure, of resolution. One who's satisfied has nothing more to do, to look for: he's already done. Whereas one who receives some stimuli is driven to move, and if the stimuli are productive then the result of his movement may be the creation of something new, something that wasn't there before but that now comes to life and possibly develops in unpredictable directions, and goes its own way, a way different from that of its fathers.

C: If you'll allow an outsider's intrusion, there seems to be a remarkable affinity between these two attitudes toward models—the one that wants them "satisfying" and the one that wants them "stimulating"—and the very models you're discussing.

A: Indeed! Theoretical elaboration is an activity, too, and in this case, too, one can inquire about the pleasure accompanying it.

B: Or *not* accompanying it. I'm sorry, but I can't have any fun in this confusion. Shall we leave the metalanguage alone and return to our original problem? What is the model that you, Angelo, consider more suggestive?

A: The one that lets me situate myself in a wider space and face more general problems—problems that initially were entirely outside our horizon but gradually, inevitably, one step after the other, one question after the other, end up imposing themselves and demanding our attention.

B: Give me an example.

A: Coming right up. We started out speaking of works of art and of the pleasure felt while contemplating one. We inquired about the origin of this pleasure and answered by invoking first understanding and then, more specifically, the *activity* of understanding. The problem of aesthetic pleasure was thus generalized to that of the pleasure felt in any activity whatsoever, so we moved to considering two hypotheses concerning the solution of *the latter* problem: one that associates the pleasure directly with the activity, and one that sees it instead as the emotional counterpart of a *state* the activity at most helps realize—a state of absence of tension, of quiet. At this point it's natural for me to ask a question that is miles away from Piero's *Resurrection*, but for which I still want an answer—and I want it, mind you, precisely on the basis of these theoretical models. The question is: which model lets me explain better the fact that people (or even animals, for that matter) act, move, do anything?

B: That's all? Don't you think you're wandering too far afield?

A: No, because we're no longer speaking only of paintings, and hence it's fair to get to the level of generality our discourse requires.

B: I begin to see what you mean by "stimulating" and "productive."

A: Good. So let's take an individual A, and suppose that A spends some of his time walking back and forth. We can imagine that A, by walking like this, resolves some existential problem, for example finds the food he needs to survive. Question: what sort of structure must we assume in *A* to explain the fact that he moves?

B: The answer seems clear. *A* moves because he needs to eat; hence he must know of this need, and know that moving will help him satisfy it.

A: And why should he do something that helps him satisfy a need?

B: What sort of question is that? Because satisfying a need is better than not satisfying it.

A: Try to be more precise. Do you mean that, every time a state of affairs *s* is "better" than the current state of affairs *t*, *A* will try to realize *s*? And in what sense "better"?

B: Let's say then that satisfying a need is pleasurable, and not satisfying it can be painful.

A: So the spring that moves *A*, for you, is pleasure?

B: I'd say yes.

A: Let's ask ourselves how this spring works, then. According to the first model, things should go more or less as follows. *A* receives a set of stimuli that disturb his quiet, for example metabolic ones. Ingesting a certain amount of food would eliminate the stimuli and let *A* return to the peace he aspires to—which would cause him pleasure. But to ingest food one must find it, and to find it one must move. So *A* decides to move, that is, to perform an activity that by itself is not at all pleasurable but can lead him to the realization of his goals, and hence to a state of pleasure.

B: It seems an accurate reconstruction of a totally reasonable proposal. Do you think there is something wrong with it?

A: It's difficult to answer your question unless we formulate an alternative and make a comparison. In sum, according to this first model, what moves *A* is an application of the *practical syllogism*: I want *s*, I know that doing *t* is a necessary condition to obtain *s*, so I do *t*. Which in turn presupposes fairly sophisticated intellectual abilities, ranging from logical reasoning to an imagination enabling one to anticipate the consequences of a given behavior.

B: And what's strange about that? We may assume that *A* has such abilities.

A: *A* may indeed have them. But a child, an ant, a chicken? They move, too; they, too, feel pleasure; maybe they, too, move *because* they feel pleasure.

B: That seems an extravagant hypothesis. Leaving aside the child, who's a somewhat special case, I don't see the reason for attributing such rational forms of behavior to ants and chickens. What's wrong with the traditional idea that animals act by instinct?

A: Nothing, except that it provides no information whatever: it states a problem rather than solving it. Why did the ant do *x*? Because it has an instinct to do *x*. Unless one says more about it, unless one articulates in detail how this "instinct" works, one will have obtained the brilliant result of explaining *obscurum per obscurius*, as when one used to say that certain things burned because there was phlogiston in them.

B: I agree, but elaborating a theory of instinct is not a problem for philosophers. The phlogiston hypothesis was bad science, and to replace it some scientific progress was needed. Analogously, to answer the questions you're interested in, we must turn to psychologists, and if they have nothing to say we must wait until their discipline has gone far enough.

A: That's certainly one way to put it, which, however, by delaying our decision indefinitely lets us sleep soundly for the moment. Another way to put it, however, *my* way, is as follows. Philosophy is where one articulates one's logical space and determines what is possible and what is not, which questions deserve an answer and which must be rejected as senseless. Insofar as science moves within logical space and uses the language philosophy has prepared for it, it will be deeply conditioned, primarily because it won't be able to take seriously a hypothesis that philosophy considered absurd.

B: I'm already familiar with these general opinions of yours. Would you mind applying them to our specific case?

A: Not at all. If the logic of action obeys the scheme we were talking about—awareness of a goal, application of the practical syllogism, and so on—then acting will be limited to beings with the required intellectual abilities. To all others action will be denied, not because we *found out* that they don't act but because we concluded that acting is *impossible* for them. When they move *as if* they acted, we'll have to eliminate this misleading *appearance* and find an alternative categorization of their behavior. The deep hiatus thus created between a man's and a camel's running constitutes, I believe, the core of the "essential" separation between mind and body, which has caused so many difficulties in our discipline—first among them that of explaining how two such deeply different realities can be mutually "coordinated," or indeed communicate with one another. It wasn't by chance that you said, earlier, that the child is "a somewhat special case." For the child is born an ant and at some point, inexplicably, must become a man (or a woman).

B: So, for you, the solution of this typical Cartesian aporia . . .

A: Not its *solution*, but its *elimination*. I don't think that this problem, like an exercise in a physics book, can be solved by an appropriate application of the theory. In my opinion, it's rather the theory that causes the problem; indeed, this is less a problem than what Kuhn would call an anomaly, and the only real "solution" to an anomaly is changing the theory.

B: That is, moving to a logical space that gives a different conceptualization of action.

A: Exactly: a logical space where the paradigm of an agent is the ant, not the philosopher.

C: I must say that, when you give examples, you always choose them very similar to yourselves. Ants, chickens, camels: all "flat," unattractive animals. Why not grasshoppers, or mandrills?

A: Possibly because, when one uses all of one's imagination in a given direction, one doesn't have much left for other purposes. But let's return to our individual *A*, and suppose that *A* has none of the intellectual abilities cited earlier, *for example* because he's an animal like an ant, or a grasshopper.

C: Thank you for your consideration.

A: You're very welcome. Suppose also that *A* moves, that by moving he finds food, that this activity somehow causes pleasure, and that the pleasure it causes is somehow responsible for the activity itself.

B: It seems you're trying to square the circle.

A: Not necessarily. Not if you admit that *A* feels pleasure precisely in *moving*, in covering certain distances, in shifting from one place to another according to certain schemes.

B: But you're talking about a play movement—one that is an end in itself. How can you extend this explanation to the case of functional movement? What guarantees that *A*, moving for the sake of moving, won't starve to death?

A: Nothing guarantees it. And I suspect that it's just the desire to provide this theoretical guarantee that has convinced most people to embrace the first model. There, apparently, rationality dominates, and what's rational seems also necessary. Here instead there are no certainties to offer, but at most a statistical regularity: that by moving in certain ways in a certain environment one will *often* end up surviving.

B: Do you mean that *A* finds food *by chance*?

A: Yes, in a sense. It finds it because it's learned genetically certain behavioral sequences, and because behaving in these ways in general leads—in the environments where A's species is adaptive—to finding food and consuming it.

B: But isn't that what one ordinarily understands by "instinct"?

A: Maybe. But there is a deep logical difference. Whereas instinctive behavior was traditionally a receptacle for everything that could *not* be regarded as action, what I'm offering you is precisely a way of conceptualizing action. That means I won't postulate a different working structure for beings *having* imagination and reason: they, too, when they act, act in the same way, repeating more or less consolidated practices *because they're the practices they are, not* because they achieve certain goals or produce *ataraxia*.

B: And pleasure, then?

A: It's the pleasure of performing those practices: the pleasure of moving, of walking, and if you will of chewing and swallowing, too; not, however, of the physical *state* that follows upon chewing and swallowing but rather of the chewing and swallowing themselves.

B: And you think that this second model is superior to the first one?

A: Superior at least in this sense: it doesn't force us to assume as many "high" intellectual functions, and hence can be extended without strain from men to microorganisms, and from adults to infants.

B: At the cost of giving up all the uniqueness and dignity of human life: our capacity to *plan* the future, to perform goal-directed actions, to exercise an intentional control over the world and over history. But I already know you will say that plans for the future are only stories told to rationalize the past—what we already did. And I don't want to get involved in these general matters, where I know by experience that you move much more skilfully than I do. I'd rather stick to specifics and ask you the same question I asked Carletto earlier—a question for which I've still received no answer, despite all the time and energy we've invested and the conceptual revolutions we've gone through. Would you mind telling me why everyday activities are indifferent to us, if indeed we perform them just for the sake of performing them? Why is listening to music fun, and shopping not?

A: Interesting question, but I'm not sure it's relevant.

B: What do you mean, "relevant"? What are we talking about?

A: We're talking about *pleasure*, not *fun*.

B: You won't get away like this, by playing with words. When I said "fun," I clearly meant "pleasure," and if you want I can reformulate the question so as to prevent you from resorting to such cheap tricks.

A: Easy, easy, let's not get upset. I haven't yet earned your trust!

B: As much trust in your intellect as you want. As for the use you make of it, however, it's best to keep a close eye on you.

A: Maybe, but in this case I was trying, in somewhat provocative terms . . .

B: Not just "somewhat," I'd say.

A: O.K., then provocative, period. But I was trying to make a distinction that I judge essential to finding our bearings in such a confused field.

B: That is?

A: Suppose I take the car to go to work, any day of the week. I open the door, sit down, turn the key, put it in first gear, let out the clutch, and start. I do all these things automatically; I've repeated them day after day, identically, for years. But I can't deny that they're always accompanied by not unpleasant emotional resonances: an accomplice's awareness of the precise point at which the stickshift offers resistance, a familiarity that verges on affection for the unspeakable confusion on the back-seat, an easy, velvety—I would almost say "elegant"—flowing of precise, effective moves, to which the vehicle responds just as predictably and functionally.

C: No question about it: you are a true fetishist. Did you ever consider what your car means for you psychologically?

A: Yes, but that's not the point now. The point is that we all experience similar sensations, that we ordinarily pay no attention to them—perhaps just because of how common they are—and that it would be entirely reasonable to call them sensations *of pleasure* if it weren't for the confusion I was trying to bring out earlier.

B: The one between pleasure and fun?

A: Exactly. Fun is something amusing, jocular, and hence also marginal, not serious: a sporting activity, a diversion. Fun is leaving the usual path of one's life. For a person working in a bank, it may be dancing, and for a dancer it might be working in a bank for a day.

C: I doubt it. Maybe an hour . . .

A: O.K. Maybe working in a bank is so trivial and repetitive that after an hour it's already become a routine. But the idea is still sound: fun is what is not (or not yet) routine.

B: And hence it's fun to do.

A: Here comes the confusion again. What you really mean . . .

B: Yes, yes, tell me what I really mean.

A: I'm sorry. Then *I* in your place would have said that what is not (yet) routine causes pleasure, not that it's fun: that it's fun is virtually tautological, given what "fun" means.

B: All right; so let's say that it causes pleasure. The substance remains the same.

A: If it makes sense to speak of substance. In any case the problem is not this hypothetical notion of substance; it's rather that, protected by the quasi-tautology "novelty is fun," one performs a delicate and tendentious ideological operation. The tautology remains such: implicitly, people keep thinking of fun as something special, something for holidays. But at the same time, because of the semantic shift between fun and pleasure, the sentence acquires more and more the meaning of "novelty causes pleasure." With two negative consequences. First, *this* sentence, too, comes to be felt as a tautology, and hence as a truth that requires no explanation. Second, it gets more and more inconceivable, illogical, that entirely normal, everyday activities might cause pleasure, and hence the emotions they generate are either named something else or go without a name at all. And we know that what has no name often ends up losing reality, too.

B: Don't you think that if this reality were so obvious it would impose itself on our attention, with or without a name?

A: I didn't say that it was obvious, or that it had enough strength to impose itself on anything. It's a subdued, bashful, elusive reality, whose voice is not easy to hear . . .

B: It sounds like you're talking about a pretty girl . . .

A: I won't deny that I'm fascinated by this reality, but I'm trying to say that you are, too, that it accompanies all our wanderings like a distant but faithful echo, and that if it did not accompany them we might very well stop.

B: Really!

A: Yes. See: I admit that novelty causes more pleasure than everyday life. This is however, for me, a contingent judgment—specifically, a contingently true one—which I don't intend to seal off by introducing a relation of pseudo-synonymy, but rather to analyze and understand in depth. At the same time, it also seems important to bring out forms of pleasure that are less intense but no less authentic, whose importance we might feel only when we lose them.

C: If they take your car away from you . . .

A: I see how you can laugh about it, but I do miss activities like driving or doing the dishes, and do find excuses to indulge in them again. Since I can't read your minds, I don't know whether you feel anything like this, and you will always be able to say that I'm the one who's not normal. But some behavioral phenomena seem to prove me right.

B: Which ones?

A: For example, the so-called *in vacuo* activities of many animals. After going without hunting mice for a while, a cat, *even if it's not hungry*, will start hunting for nothing, and its appearance will strongly suggest that what it's doing gives it intense pleasure.

B: It's easy to get out of trouble by referring to cats and mice, since they can't contradict you.

A: It's not verification or evidence that I need. You have challenged me to account within my model for the fact that ordinary activities cause no pleasure. And I'm trying to respond to the challenge, which doesn't require me to convince you of the correctness of the model but only of its compatibility with the "fact" you cited.

B: But you're denying this fact!

A: I'm not denying it, but certainly I'm reformulating it. What seems undeniable to me is that ordinary activities don't cause as much pleasure as the *extra*ordinary, cathartic, holiday ones. A little pleasure, I noted, they do seem to cause, and maybe if we were more careful in using the word "pleasure" we would realize it. It does remain true, however, that watching a play or listening to a piece of music is more pleasurable than driving . . .

C: Thank God you admit that!

A: . . . and it's *this* truth that I believe I must—and can—explain.

B: So far you haven't explained it, though.

A: With all your interruptions, it's no wonder it takes me a long time. But now I have brought out enough elements to proceed quickly.

B: Seeing you proceed quickly would sure be a holiday pleasure.

A: Jokes aside, I've already made clear that my model is an adaptive-evolutionistic one, where pleasure directly accompanies an activity to the extent that this activity, in the environment to which a species is adapted, *often* proves functional to the species' survival. Now it's natural to supplement this model as follows: the more important an activity is for the survival of the species, the more pleasure will be felt in performing it.

B: You must explain in what sense looking at an abstract painting is useful to the species' survival. I would understand if we were speaking of orgasm.

A: Exactly. Indeed, this thesis has often been stated in connection with feeding or reproduction. But when we move to aesthetic pleasure things get complicated, and to solve the complications one often babbles about some other kind of pleasure, a more spiritual or elevated one, creating once more specious dichotomies to resolve the problems caused by inadequate conceptual schemes.

B: As was the case with mind and body?

A: Right! And this is more than a superficial analogy: it's the same absurd theory of action that gives trouble in both cases. When an action is defined in terms of achieving a goal, and seen as motivated by the pleasure accompanying this *result*, it's easy to account for the structure of actions like eating or copulating . . .

B: Less easy, maybe, in cases of obesity or perversion.

A: To be sure, and the defense against such cases is usually an attack, that is, an accusation of "abnormality." Whereas one can think one has categorized the normal cases satisfactorily . . .

B: Except that there are very few normal cases.

A: Certainly, but at least there's an alibi, however weak and naive. With aesthetic pleasure, however, the alibi doesn't work. What result is obtained through the contemplation of a work of art? What does one get by spending one's time around museums?

B: Sometimes, a salary.

A: To put it this way would be a step in the right direction, but it would eventually lead us to blame the whole practice of art appreciation on some kind of institutional bad faith—a fraud not only widespread but even necessary for the very existence of this form of life. And one needs courage to maintain such heterodox opinions, more courage than most philosophers have.

C: Or they wouldn't be philosophers.

A: Probably. So one prefers to talk about a *meaning* to be captured, a *message* to be interpreted, an *ideal form* to be perceived, and since meanings, messages, and forms are not things we stumble over, one also invents a component of our being that enjoys "consuming" such stuff.

B: Rather than inventing it, if I understand you correctly, one uses it, since it was already invented for other purposes.

A: What the original purpose was I don't know. But, once it's there, this entity proves very useful for a great number of tasks, for filling all sorts of conceptual gaps . . .

B: Now don't get carried away by rhetoric. You still need to explain what function *you* assign to this "aesthetic activity." Do you intend to adopt the heterodox attitude mentioned earlier? Have you got more courage than most philosophers?

A: I don't think so. My solution is much more traditional, and consistent with all I said so far. If an action, a practice, is characterized not as a behavior dictated by a conscious purpose, but as a system of moves that prove functional because they're generally integrated with the environment where they're performed, and promote there the survival of the species, then the adaptive significance of the aesthetic practice will indeed have to be found in its *general* effects, that is, not in something that every particular employment of this practice obtains for us, but in the advantages of having such a practice available and constantly activating it in given circumstances.

B: All this is quite abstract. Could you give an example?

A: Sure. In fact, I'll give you two, at the two extremes of a spectrum of possible forms of behavior, as it were. First example: For reasons we're presently not interested in, you are lost in an unfamiliar forest and are not able to survive there. So you must find a way out; but this is very difficult because the environment is confusing: there are no paths or indications of any kind, only trees and bushes all around you, all apparently identical to one another. For some time you wander with no sense of direction: you don't understand the logic, the structure of this situation, and you know that you *must* understand it if you are to survive. Then, eventually, after a lot of effort, you begin to recognize certain elements, certain patterns; you realize that a certain series of steps takes you back to the same point; hence to avoid always returning to that point you must deviate either to the right or to the left, and so on. If you go far enough in thus mastering your surroundings, I'd almost say in establishing a *dialogue* with the forest, in *understanding* its *language*, your life is saved.

C: Thank God!

A: Second example: You're here in front of this *Resurrection*, prey to conflicting, lively feelings, aware that the painting is "telling" you something but not quite able to understand what it is. You look at Christ's face, at his eyes staring yet not fixed on anything specific, at the flag that doesn't wave because there's no wind, at the bodies of the "witnesses" to this supernatural act, abandoned to a sleep very much like death, and ask yourself: What's the logic of the situation? Why is the episode represented like this?

C: Which is what I was trying to say earlier: what does the author want to communicate?

A: Yes, it's what you were saying earlier. I don't intend to contradict you but, if you don't mind, to generalize your hypotheses a bit.

C: It remains to be seen *why* they should be generalized.

A: Because, if we limit ourselves to saying that aesthetic experience consists in understanding a message, we can't explain why in the world it's pleasurable.

C: And you can?

A: I'm trying to. So in this case, as in the previous one of the forest, your first reaction is disorientation, and what follows might be an attempt to unravel the mystery. In this case, too, you will only get to the bottom of it by establishing certain connections and recognizing certain regularities. For example, you will notice that neither Christ nor his custodians (for different reasons) look at each other—indeed, none of them looks at anything—and that Christ's lack of expression is reflected and duplicated in the unconsciousness of the four soldiers. You will inquire about the reasons for this regularity, and might conjecture that such an expression of indifference is a sign of absolute *foreignness*: in the same way, if you "met" an ant . . .

C: Here we go again with ants . . .

A: . . . neither of you would pay special attention to the other, at least not to the point of trying to *communicate* something. But this foreignness will cause you problems. What, you will say, wasn't Christ resurrected *for us*, to save us, to save even these four poor sleeping wrecks? And then you might begin to realize the deep significance of this painting, and the reason for the fascination it exercised, somewhat obscurely, on you. For, as a natural answer to your perplexities, you might come to understand the work as an expression of the *cosmic risk* connected with salvation. Christ will pass by us, but will we be awake enough to see him? He belongs to another reality, to a windless world where flags don't wave: will we be able to recognize him under the appearance he will have chosen? We can't expect him to stop, to attract our attention, to express himself in our language. He will probably just go his way, impassible, inexorable, and missing him then will mean missing him forever.

B: Quite a merciless image of Christianity.

A: And I'm not implying that it's a correct image. But it does allow me to orient myself with respect to this fresco, to overcome my initial wonder and embarrassment, to rationalize my feelings.

B: However interesting, this interpretation doesn't seem deeply different—not in style, at least—from the one Carletto proposed for the *Flagellation*. If I understand you correctly, the difference should emerge from juxtaposing it with the previous example of being lost in the forest.

A: That's right. For they have much in common. In both cases, an individual finds himself in a strange situation, one he's not used to, one he does not understand—which means essentially: one he can't handle with ease. In both, the individual does his best to penetrate the logic of the situation, to identify some regularities in it and to explain them, until, one step at a time, the situation becomes familiar and he learns to move without difficulty. In both, the outcome of this activity consists in internalizing a "map" of the situation, understood as a system of answers to counterfactual questions: what would happen if I turned right, or went straight ahead, or the guards opened their eyes, or the flag waved?

C: Yes, what would happen if the flag waved?

A: Probably, Christ would enter *our* world and it would be easier to recognize him.

B: Just a moment, never mind the details. You mean that the pleasure connected with the appreciation of a work of art—where this appreciation amounts to understanding the message evoked by the work, or internalizing the relevant "map"—must be explained by relating it to the adaptive value of the practice "how to find one's way in a new, strange, and embarrassing situation, and gradually learn to control it."

A: Yes, that is precisely what I mean. And you'll see that this adaptive value is very high. Some have said that man's specialty is his lack of specialization; biologically, this means that his genetic programs are ready to interact with the most diverse environments and to articulate themselves in response to them—that they have room for absorbing new information. And it's just this kind of learning that I'm talking about, the kind that has made it possible for man to occupy the whole earth, from the poles to the equator, to adopt the most disparate forms of nourishment and social aggregation, to overcome natural and artificial catastrophes of enormous proportions.

B: O.K. Then it's reasonable that so useful a practice will be accompanied by a very lively pleasure. But the application of this practice to the appreciation of a work of art would seem to be a rather marginal phenomenon, a sort of play that *imitates*, but does not *reproduce*, the most "meaningful" uses of the practice. So why did this marginal use become pervasive in human history? Why did art, from a simple overflowing of energies destined for quite different (and much more important) ends, become one of the principal channels of our "research" activity?

A: Because the other channels are usually obstructed. Our lives run along predictable paths, and to keep us on them there's no need for impertinent, noisy feelings: it's quite enough to have the light, shy background of our reassuring familiarity with everydayness, of our warm, agreeable "feeling at home." When do we ever find ourselves in a forest, dealing with mysterious dangers, we normal people I mean, not missionaries or mercenaries or the boldest entrepreneurs?

B: Maybe when we're competing for a job.

A: Maybe, but even then nothing much is mysterious or needs to be understood. There are hurt feelings, of course, but one knows why, one knows it from the beginning. So a form of life of fundamental biological importance and a source of pleasure among the richest and most intense are blocked, dried up. Your reference to play is very appropriate: in a normal life, people explore, discover, and learn only until they grow up, until the end of adolescence. Once that is over, the most productive sort of behavior is also the most rigid, the one that follows instructions to the letter . . .

B: A computer's behavior, in sum.

A: Yes, unfortunately. And hence also the sort of behavior that leaves the least room for play, for experiment, for research. When one gets to this point, there's nothing more to learn: one need only execute. So aesthetic experience provides the most concrete possibility of recovering, in part, this playful but also intellectual aspect of our lives, this widening of our boundaries denied by everyday efficiency.

B: As drugs do for some, or a casino's green tables . . .

A: . . . or maniacal traveling, or constant bed-hopping. All forms of behavior animated, in the end, by the same restlessness, and supported by the same hope: that of meeting the challenge posed by novelty, whether large or small, and of *enjoying* the adventure.

B: I understand.

C: I don't. I *thought* I understood, and I even thought I agreed, but the more you speak the crazier your position sounds . . .

A: Why?

C: I don't find it easy to express myself at the level of generality you guys are used to; but I can think of many concrete problems. Take this one, for example. I find myself walking in the Piazza del Santo in Padua, and see the equestrian statue of Gattamelata, a work of Donatello. In what sense is this a strange or embarrassing experience? Don't I recognize immediately that it's a man on horseback? What else do I need in order to construct a "map" of the situation? And do I perhaps feel less pleasure for this reason?

A: Why? The horsemen you ordinarily run into are made of bronze?

C: Don't try to be funny. Horsemen are not, but statues of horsemen are.

A: All right. But why couldn't this very ambiguity be the decisive element? Suppose it's true, as some theorize, that art was born when primitive people began to "see" familiar shapes in accidental marks on the walls of their caves, and were so fascinated by them that they started drawing marks and reproducing shapes themselves. Then this might very well be what matters: recognizing *something* in *something else*, learning to dominate the intrinsically destabilizing situation in which an object, without ceasing to be itself, begins also to "stand for" another object, and thus forces us to a periodic oscillation, a continuous uncertainty.

C: You will admit that in some cases there isn't much oscillation.

A: Sure, I admit it. In the presence of the Gattamelata statue, it's difficult today to remember that it's *also* the result of a casting, and recreate the shock waves that must have run through its contemporaries as they witnessed that almost magical operation, which, from opaque, inert metal, had extracted the perfect image of a man. The ease with which today we can reproduce any reality has eventually trivialized this feeling, and chocked it.

C: It's precisely here that I can't follow you. Your conception of aesthetic pleasure seems very much on target for *certain* works. Take the *Pietà Rondanini*, and consider the labor, the pain with which its figures struggle against the marble, not to be swallowed by it, not to lose their individuality. A work like this does seem to be characterized by the ambiguity, the tension you're talking about, and fits your theory perfectly. What I don't understand is why this theory should then be stretched to cover cases that do not fit it, that indeed contradict it, like that of Donatello's statue. Why should we insist on looking for ambiguity and tension in what is rather a paradigm of classical composure, of balance, of rigor? Why should we fantasize about its contemporaries' reactions? Indeed, who cares about its contemporaries? *Even if* they had received the work as you say, as something magical, etcetera, does that mean that *we now* can no longer enjoy it, that the subsequent technological developments have denied us this pleasure forever?

B: It doesn't seem that his position allows for any alternative here; indeed, he himself spoke earlier of trivializing, and eventually chocking, certain feelings.

C: And this, if I may say so, is absurd. I believe I can enjoy Donatello as much as, or even more than, one of his contemporaries.

B: Not to mention the fact that on this view the universal character of works of art goes by the wayside. Instead of an "absolute" aesthetic value, we should perhaps talk of aesthetic value "in a situation," that is, relative to specific individuals and environments.

C: Yes, and maybe we'll discover that the *present* aesthetic value of a song by Madonna—considering how primitive its listeners are—is equivalent to the *Renaissance* value of the Gattamelata statue.

A: Wait a minute, I beg you. If you don't stop, you won't leave a stone standing here. I realize that we got to a very delicate point, where several reasons for misunderstanding come together . . .

C: No, no, what misunderstanding? We understand you perfectly well. It's just that you're wrong.

A: Maybe, but before pronouncing your verdict you might give me a chance to defend myself.

C: Go ahead.

A: Let me begin with a general statement. I don't like the idea that a theory—aesthetic or otherwise—is good for certain cases but not for others, for which we need a different theory. There exists in us, Kant would say, an irresistible tendency to systematicity, which finds such a "division of labor" repulsive. Rather than accepting it, I would prefer to abandon my theory.

C: We would have no problem with that.

A: I'm sure. But I don't think I have to abandon it, at least not because of your objections. Which objections, by the way, I could easily turn against you, for it seems undeniable that there are oscillations of taste from one age to another, that works once extremely popular are often entirely forgotten, and then sometimes rediscovered when taste changes again.

B: You won't tell me now that popularity is the index of the value of a work?

A: Not the only index, to be sure. I agree with Carletto that this value is also a function of the risks the work takes, of how much it tries to overcome triviality and communicate a sophisticated, interesting content. *Communicate* it, though, not simply express it. An author writes in order to be read, a painter paints so that his paintings will be looked at, a composer composes music so that it's played to an audience; without this at least ideal presence of an interlocutor, it would be difficult to distinguish an artist from a madman confabulating with himself.

B: Indeed, sometimes the barriers are shaky.

A: I know, but that, too, must be explained. Just as one must explain, not simply state, the fact that the value of a work depends on its level of complexity. And one must clarify the relation between this complexity and the "institutional" need to establish a dialogue with the public.

C: All of which is brilliantly clarified by your theory, I imagine.

A: I don't know how brilliantly, but the attempt to clarify it is there. An attempt ultimately based, once more, on the previous analysis of action. Traditionally, as we have seen, the concept of intention was crucial for understanding human behavior. Man only acts when he *wants* to act in a certain way, usually to attain certain goals; otherwise his behavior is not action, it's just something that *happens*. In particular, when the artist communicates something to a public, it's because he wants to, and the public understands only if it understands *what* the artist wants to communicate.

C: And how else could it be?

A: Try for an instant to see things from my point of view. The artist moves in a certain way because he's received from tradition a "vocabulary" of practices and takes pleasure in applying them, in manipulating clay or marble or words according to certain stylistic criteria, trying every now and then to force the criteria in slightly (or very) new directions—much as a child loves to play in the backyard but also, sometimes, to explore the woods nearby. In a situation like this, can we still speak of the *meaning* of what the artist does? Is it possible to speak of a process of *communication*?

C: I don't see how. Your artist reminds me of an indeterministic automaton.

A: But it *is* possible, if one turns one's attention from the artist to the public, and finds the *conceptual location* of meaning in the latter.

C: What do you have in mind?

A: That the notion of meaning will be defined on the basis of the notion of a public, that meaning will be something that a public determines, and that if the public changes then different meanings, or even no meaning at all, could be determined for the same work.

C: Try to be more precise. How does this determination come about?

A: Through the public's capacity to orient itself with respect to the work, to react to it, and to control it. A work like this, like the *Resurrection* I mean, might cause the observer, for the most diverse reasons (maybe even because it was discussed in books on art history), instability and embarrassment. Some will react to these feelings by placing Piero della Francesca within his time frame, and speaking of his linear perspective and his sense of color; others will go psychological, insisting on Piero's identification with one of the sleepers; still others will try to read the painting as a text, to reduce it to a statement, as I did earlier when I spoke of salvation. Each such reaction lets the observer situate himself with respect to the work, integrate it into his own personality, and find what it means *for him*.

C: And each reaction is as good as any other, if I understand. *Including* the reaction of someone who says: "Piero's perspective is outdone by photographic reproduction techniques, so Piero has nothing more to tell me." This guy, too, is "situating himself" with respect to the work and "integrating it"—or rather, disintegrating it—into his own personality. He, too, has found *his* meaning of the *Resurrection*.

A: Exactly.

C: It may be exact for you, but I find it silly. A theory pretending to account for aesthetic experience and unable to discriminate among these attitudes should have the guts to declare bankruptcy.

A: You're moving too fast. I never said that my theory can't make such discriminations. But, instead of making them on the basis of a hypothetical absolute value of the work of art, I will—as indeed Bertoldo figured out—relativize them to the person considering the work, and find criteria of judgment and value *internal* to his situation.

C: Look, you may be saying something extraordinary but I'm not following you. If you really want me to get it, answer this question: Why, on the basis of your theory, *should* someone (and notice the normative aspect of my formulation) stop devoting all his time to B movies and supermarket tabloids, and commit himself with labor and sweat to under- standing—or, if you prefer, "controlling"—Beethoven's Fifth or *Guer- nica*? Why, if B movies and supermarket tabloids already give him plea- sure? Those who speak of the "hypothetical absolute value" of a work of art have an answer: because the Fifth has a higher value, a function of its content and of the great stylistic mastery it expresses. But if we turn our attention to the public, to its reactions, to what it understands or likes, can we still find an answer?

A: Sure; indeed we can find a couple. In general—or, to put it *à la* Ross, *prima facie*—it's better to labor to understand the Fifth than to rest content with B movies because the Fifth makes available to us an addi- tional source of enjoyment, and probably a different kind of enjoyment, too.

C: I'm still not following.

A: Let's begin with the *prima facie*. What I mean—and what Ross meant when he spoke of *prima facie duties*—is that a theory can only provide you with abstract judgments, and it's for you to apply them to concrete cases—assuming all the relevant risks. A theory will say: doing *X* is *in general* better than not doing it, or better than doing *Y*. In a specific situation, many of these judgments will be applicable, and you won't be able to apply them all. You'll have to choose *which* of the many things that it's better to do you *want* to do, to which of the many values the situation brings out you want to lend your ear. In particular, even if you had concluded that listening to Beethoven is better than listening to

Madonna, it's entirely possible that in some cases, given how much you've already invested in other matters, you'll end up choosing Madonna *and no one will have a right to criticize you.*

B: Here you go again with your separation of theory and practice. So what's the point of having a theory?

A: I've already answered this question . . .

C: Wait a minute! Leave your general discussion of theories for another time, and don't change the subject right now—just when I'm beginning to understand something. You've explained the *prima facie*, Angelo; now explain the rest.

A: But of course. See, I'm convinced that a work like the *Resurrection* offers not just one but many opportunities for enjoyment. One of these I find it natural to call *aesthetic*, primarily because—in our social situation, where as we noted there isn't much encouragement for play and exploration—it seems most specifically relevant to artistic objects and experiences. But after all it's only a verbal matter. What's important is that there are numerous ways of deriving pleasure from Piero.

C: No doubt about it. But many are wrong.

A: I envy your confidence. As far as I'm concerned, they're just different. Among them, at any rate, there's also the one that consists in repeating, in front of this work, words already said before, and one can't deny that this kind of behaviour has positive and pleasurable aspects. It's certainly reassuring, it provides us with an expert's reputation, we wear it like a comfortable shoe . . .

B: Like the car you were talking about earlier.

A: Right: there's the same familiarity, the same warmth, the same tenderness here.

C: So the critic would be some sort of Linus wrapped in his blanket.

A: That's not what I said. I didn't use the word "critic," but rather "expert." And a critic is not only an expert: he's also someone who devotes much more time than the average person to artistic objects and thus may be better equipped to overcome the commonplaces of tradition.

C: You really hate tradition!

A: Not at all. To say "commonplace" for me is not to make an objection. Commonplaces are consolidated, safe practices, which we can trust and to which we must turn whenever we're under environmental pressure—which for most of us is the rule. It's only under very special conditions of material ease that some people can afford the luxury of going beyond commonplaces.

C: For the others, then, let there be Madonna!

A: Yes, I'd say, if Madonna soothes them, if they have no trouble identifying with her simple, superficial songs . . .

C: But then what about the critic's educational function? Are you saying that he can only address other lazy bums like himself, that he can only communicate with other critics?

A: You will agree that this is what ordinarily happens. And we should reflect on what happens ordinarily, because if it does then it must be what happens most easily, and the fact that it's easy—much easier than its opposite—can teach us a lot about the structure of the situation.

C: But why should we rest content with this structure? Why shouldn't we change it?

A: I'm impressed by your "dialectical" turnabout: now you want to change the structure. I'd be happy to just understand how it works.

C: O.K., so tell me how it works.

A: I'm trying. I take pleasure in driving my car, but not only in driving my car; also, for example, in cooking or doing the dishes. Which means: even among my ordinary activities, my "commonplaces," I have more than one opportunity to do things that cause me agreeable, tender, and reassuring feelings, and in general it's better to have more such opportunities than fewer. But to have them one needs commitment: one must *learn* the desired practice, one must *make it* a commonplace. If it's something easy, or if we have a natural inclination for it, not too much commitment is required; otherwise, it will take a great deal of motivation not to lose heart in the face of boring exercises and less than brilliant results. Think of the labor it takes to master the practice of music appreciation up to the point of enjoying the *Après-midi d'un faune.*

B: Especially if you have a tin ear.

A: Exactly. And think of how few people would want to do it, unless they were forced.

C: Forced? By whom?

A: By critics, for God's sake. That is precisely where most of their educational function is to be found. By using their social prestige as leverage, they convince us that we *must* pay attention to these "difficult" phenomena, and make us feel guilty if we don't. In this way, somewhat forcibly, they contribute to extending our capacity for pleasure.

C: I don't feel very comfortable identifying with this torturer's image but, my feelings aside, your criterion seems obtusely quantitative, and as such still inadequate to account for true value judgments. It's as if you were saying—or better: as if you were making this critic–drill-sergeant of yours say—"speaking two languages is better than speaking just one, speaking three is even better, and so on," so that people, consistently with their other commitments, won't be satisfied with speaking, say, English but will also study Chinese or Russian or Arabic.

A: This comparison with languages seems right on target.

C: Thank you for the compliment, but, if you don't mind, this strategy doesn't even *address* the problem I'm interested in. I don't care whether Mahler provides me with different means of expression than Billy Ray Cyrus; I want to know whether he provides me with *better ones*.

A: You're right, but I wasn't through yet. I had mentioned not only an additional source of enjoyment but also a different *kind* of enjoyment. Now we must clarify this second remark.

C: Your procedure may be systematic, but I find it very irritating. That was my question to begin with; so why did you spend all this time talking about something *else* instead of getting right to the point?

A: By getting right to the point, as you put it, one risks giving answers *ad hoc*, which may be contradicted when new questions arise. Remember that the attack on me earlier was quite general, so to provide a proper response I must present my position in an organic way.

C: O.K., but that was the most important question for me.

A: Then you can't complain if I address it last, after providing it with an adequate context.

B: There's no hope, Carletto. Either you leave before he even begins or you have to let him speak his own way.

A: Don't be so negative, Bertoldo. After all, isn't that what everyone does, speak his own way? Returning to the issue, there are more or less elaborate, more or less expressive media, practices, styles. Once one learns to play tic-tac-toe, there's nothing left but playing one game after another, with little variation. We may well like this, but probably the same way we like driving our car, that is, as a technique we have mastered and feel at home with. Whereas with checkers, or better still with chess, it's quite a different matter: it's always possible to create new situations and surprising moves which raise problems never even *imagined* before. Well, the same holds for the practices categorized as artistic. The first time we heard a rock-and-roller venturing around notes, audaciously realizing tones a comma or two above or below what musical theory dictated, stretching his "rough" voice on dissonant chords, exploding with a falsetto well beyond the range "allowed" to him, all this created obvious difficulties for our acoustic reception—together with opportunities for exploring new avenues, for extending our vision away from the beaten paths, well into the thick "forest." In the long run, however, the game has gotten stale: a few years of experimentation have been sufficient to exhaust its capacity for expression, and to transform it—as a "sensitive soul" might have predicted—into an academic phenomenon, where consumer products as technically perfect as they're defunct match the pathetic stardom of performers whose only merit is *our own* nostalgia.

B: You have the typical attitude of a person who grew up in the Sixties: the only real music is Bob Dylan, indeed the Bob Dylan *of those days.* Aren't you being ethnocentric? Why do you want to deprive the new generations of all hope?

A: I don't know if I'm ethnocentric, but certainly I won't give up being *centered* on *my* vocabulary of feelings and experiences. I'll try to articulate it, to rationalize it, to structure it, but I won't deny it: that would be stupid. By running after neutrality I would only reach emptiness. Thus, while I don't intend to deny anyone his hopes, I won't let anyone deny *me* my opinions, or my right to systematize and defend them.

B: No one wants to deny you your rights, Angelo. It's only that . . .

A: Look, if you don't like the example find another one. The world and the history of art are full of revolutionary phenomena that suddenly arouse enthusiasm but just as easily run out of gas—meaning their capacity to cause wonder. Personally I would include futurism, photorealism, and pop art among them. And note that, when these artistic forms no longer cause wonder or stimulate our exploratory instinct, they can still make a contribution. They might still appeal to other components of our personality—for example, to the often-cited pleasure that derives from being used to something—and it's also possible that, after being dormant for a while, perhaps forgotten, they might be rediscovered, and cause wonder again. After all, each generation begins anew, and the fact that something is years or centuries old doesn't necessarily make it a commonplace—if it has been locked in a closet for a long time.

C: So in this case the critic . . .

A: . . . is someone who knows what's in the closets, and at the right time decides to bring out some piece of clothing that, just because most people don't recognize it, can still look new.

C: A rather sleazy operation!

A: Maybe, especially if carried out in cold blood. But here I'm not interested in the moral and human dimension of the individual who happens to be a critic; in particular, in his capacity to feel genuine excitement for his proposals. I'm interested in his social role, which allows for a periodical resurfacing of the "inventory" and thus prevents past efforts from going to waste.

C: Your language is a good example of a practice that insists on trying to cause wonder. But I'd prefer that we not elaborate further on subjects that still seem quite inessential. Isn't there anything else at stake in aesthetic experience, besides this mixture of obtuse repetition and *épater les bourgeois?*

A: Sure: there's the equivalent of chess, not only of tic-tac-toe.

C: You mean something *inescapably* complex?

A: Precisely, and it's interesting to get a closer look at this complexity. Suppose that White moves a pawn or a rook. This gesture, in and by itself, is a simple one, but through how many different filters it is possible to see it, into how many "plans" it is possible to insert it, to how many conflicting "intentions" it is possible to attribute it! And how hard it is to decide among all these readings! As soon as you settle on one, you notice aspects of the situation that don't quite fit it, that you didn't quite explain, and almost insensibly you slide into another point of view, another interpretation. Then, maybe, when you don't find the latter satisfactory, either, you go back to the original one and perceive there potentialities you had missed earlier, strong points that suddenly seem decisive . . .

B: Thank God I only play blitz chess!

C: One moment: now let's not start talking about chess. You make me lose my head!

A: O.K., let's leave chess aside and consider this fresco once again. We've interpreted it, we gave it what seemed a credible reading, but if we keep on looking at it we can't help feeling that we haven't totally exhausted it—indeed we have in some sense misunderstood it, betrayed it. As we observe it and compare it with our translation into words, into one or more sentences attempting to capture its message, the painting seems to rebel against this scheme, to proclaim its poverty, its one-sidedness, to propose itself as the carrier of contradictory indications, or rather of indications that will *appear* contradictory *to us*, who insist on mortifying its spirit with our cheap alphabet.

C: Could you be more concrete?

A: Sure. We spoke earlier of a historical, unrepeatable occasion, of an appointment with eternity, and of the tragic, terrifying risk of coming to this appointment unprepared, distracted by the laziness and weakness of a body too burdensome and foolish. We spoke of a superhuman vision that goes by without waking us, of our destiny inexorably, mercilessly leaving us behind, of the guilt of not having looked at the right time. And we were satisfied with all this, for a while. But then questions arise. Why are the faces of these sleepers, of one of them especially, so intent, as if they actually *saw* something? What do they see? And why does Christ move so lightly? Why don't Jericho's trumpets play at his passage? Why does his triumph have no spectators? Or does it have them, and we don't realize it? What if this vision were a *dream*, a dream of salvation and redemption for men bent under their weaknesses but still capable of a gesture of emancipation, capable at least of comparing their miserable reality with an ideal hypothesis, of evoking a different presence, a super-sensible image, which, abstract as it might be, gives sense and value to all that is concrete?

C: Quite a change from your former interpretation!

A: Yes, but a natural change when one takes a certain point of view —understood literally, that is, as a point from which to *view* the painting. Earlier I concentrated on Christ's face, on the firmness of his expression, on how much it suggests something atemporal, eternal, ineluctable, and the sleepers immediately sank to the condition of people who missed the boat, who couldn't understand the course and the meaning of history. Whereas now, as I focus my attention precisely on those sleepers, Christ recedes, moves to the background, loses concreteness and reality. There's an oscillation between two faces, as it were—Christ's and that of the man seen full face in the foreground. First one attracts us and the other almost disappears, then—for no reason but the intrinsic nature of the work—the other slowly comes forward and imposes itself. An unresolved and unre-solvable tension . . .

C: I'd say an ambiguity.

A: And you'd be right. Think of the many references to the ambiguity of Mona Lisa's smile, and of how often this ambiguity was considered a decisive factor in the fascination exercised by the painting. Quite reason-ably, for the ambiguity lets the observer project onto the work different meanings at different times, without ever finding that the work is ex-hausted and hence that the play is over, and with it the "fun"—I'd rather say the pleasure—the play affords.

C: Do you mean to say that the more ambiguous a work, the more it is aesthetically valid?

A: It's not so easy. A straight line is one of the most ambiguous things there are: it's possible to complete it in the most disparate ways. But I don't think it would generate much enthusiasm among viewers.

C: It has happened.

A: Yes, but it was the kind of stunt we've already mentioned. After a while it's forgotten.

C: Whereas with Piero . . .

A: . . . we face an extraordinary capacity for getting the observer involved and causing him to reflect, perhaps with conflicting and paradoxical outcomes but also with the sense that it was worth it. What exactly is hidden behind this capacity is difficult to say. I suspect that we haven't yet refined the necessary tools of analysis; in the future—who knows?—chaos theory might be able to help us. To be sure, several factors are involved. Technical mastery, to begin with, which certainly struck Piero's contemporaries and forced them to take the work seriously. For us, who are more used to this compositional and representational ability, a compensating element is the very history of the painting, its age, its fame: if it had been produced by a friend of ours over the weekend, we might just shrug our shoulders.

C: Think of those three boys who carved fake Modiglianis with a Black & Decker, and the big mess that followed.

A: Precisely. Nothing wrong with a bit of healthy cultural terrorism, if it makes us pay attention and stirs us from our inertia. Then we'll see how long the thing lasts, how far it goes, whether it continues to challenge us or ends up drowning us in boredom.

C: And, once more, the protagonist of this "healthy" cultural terrorism would be the critic. However much you try, there doesn't seem to be a positive role in your system for the professionals of aesthetics.

A: I don't see what's negative about it. If by a role we understand a *social* role—and clearly this is what we're talking about—what is a society if not a system of forces, pushing and pulling in different, sometimes opposite directions? And what can a "professional of aesthetics" do, except add his force to that of others, and push and pull in the direction he's interested in?

C: That is not what I meant, and you know it. The pushing and pulling is fine, but your critic seems unable to avoid a certain duplicity, a certain lack of truthfulness. He doesn't push and pull *directly*, but in oblique ways, using as leverage base feelings like the desire to be fashionable, not to be judged stupid, to increase one's prestige.

A: And you find this objectionable?

C: You mean you don't?

A: The only objectionable thing here may be the fact that we have a problem, that we find these motives "base." Or maybe not; this fact, too, after all, is part of the situation and must be explained in the same terms.

We must never forget that our individual survival depends much more on our being faithful to trusted habits than on our willingness to "play," and hence that, to make us play, one must use both carrot and stick: scare us with being culturally disqualified and let us glance from afar at a prize for our enormous (and mostly useless) labors. All this, of course, until (after quite some labor) we begin to enjoy it. Then our motivation becomes autonomous, and it becomes important to exhort us not to get carried away, not to forget our social obligations and responsibilities, not to turn into "misfits."

B: Leaving us no way out, no hope.

A: Yes, but there's nothing evil in this result. The conflictual situation we have thus reached, so painfully split between opposite demands and unable to resolve the tension one way or the other, constitutes the most effective answer to an environment that is itself dominated by tensions and conflicts, in which committing oneself entirely to one direction would involve the risk of becoming obsolete.

B: One moment. Before you start with your daring biological metaphors, let me return to our problem.

A: Be my guest.

B: If things are as you say, what justifies the duplicity and the bad faith? The task accomplished by aesthetic experience is an important one: it guarantees us a certain amount of mental elasticity. So why not just tell people how things are? Why tell them stories about other tasks supposedly accomplished by this experience? Indeed, it seems that there is here a *double* duplicity, a *triple* purpose. There's what aesthetic experience is really good for (the biological motivation), what *one says* it is good for (idle talk concerning its spiritual value), and the reasons why people get involved in it (prestige, blackmail, and so on), without confessing it even to themselves. Why so many complications?

A: Because pain motivates more effectively than pleasure, so much so that it has often supplanted it conceptually.

B: What do you mean?

A: I'm referring to the two models of pleasure we discussed earlier. One, as you recall, made it consist in quieting down tensions, stimuli, conflicts—all disturbing things, which in extreme situations can cause pain. For this model, pleasure simply means cessation or absence of pain, and hence it has no independent dignity, no specific significance.

B: Whereas in the other model . . .

A: In the other model there remains the possibility of doing something to escape painful stimuli, but there is also an alternative route: that of carrying out an activity because *carrying it out, acting* in a certain way, causes pleasure.

B: But this route can be reduced to the other one. We need only think that *not* performing a given activity constitutes an *internal* source of painful stimuli for certain organisms.

A: The reduction is certainly possible, and even desirable for conceptual economy. But it's still true that, in this behavioral model, we emphasize the organism's *autonomy*, the independence of some of its motivations, whereas in the other one we picture it as purely reactive, moving only in response to (unpleasant) environmental solicitations and trying to escape them. I agree that, when the organism gets complex enough, analogous solicitations will come from the inside, too, possibly accumulating and then periodically exploding, and I also agree that by this structural complication we can (and perhaps must) explain everything in the organism's behavior that seems dominated by intrinsic, self-sufficient rules. But aside from these possible (or even necessary) theoretical reductions there are also ideological tendencies—often encouraged and supported by simple shifts of emphasis, by the use of paradigmatic examples, maybe even the choice of key terms. It is *my* ideological tendency, then, to insist precisely on the levels of autonomy reached by the organism, and to say that, if even they *originated from* a purely reactive state, *by now* they're no longer part of that state.

B: But, if I understand you correctly, favoring the more passive model is not just an ideological choice. You also said that pleasure doesn't provide very effective motivations.

A: Not as effective as the cessation of pain. Why? Because pain presents itself with urgency: when something hurts, it hurts *now* and makes us act *right away*. With the "autonomous" activities I'm talking about, the situation is quite different. We may even get to the point where, if we don't spend enough time performing one of them, we'll face unpleasant endogenous stimuli, but it usually takes a while to get to that point: we must have practiced the activity for some time, exercised our ability quite a bit, and thus transformed the activity into something that comes naturally. *Before* all this, there may be at most an undifferentiated uneasiness, a generic discontent, a sense of throwing away our time, but no specific drive to move in a certain way. So the problem is how to *reach* that point, how to get a person to take the steps needed for a given activity to *begin* to come naturally, and this problem is solved by regressing to the more primitive (and safer) motivational scheme. That is, one creates for the organism some *external* disturbing elements, and hopes that, by making it move to escape these elements, it will develop the *internal* sources of stimuli necessary for autonomous behavior (and for deriving pleasure from such behavior).

B: And the external disturbing elements would include social blackmail?

A: Exactly: they would include making people feel embarrassed if they don't do or understand or appreciate certain things.

B: O.K., but what about the other fraudulent motivation? Why is it necessary to elaborate on the deep significance and great nobility of art works? To be quite frank about it, it's this kind of talk that takes me in, for it makes me think that there's something there I missed entirely. Whereas, if you're right, there's nothing at all, or at least nothing of that kind.

A: I'm not sure that there's nothing of that kind. As I see it, it's legitimate to say that an art work communicates a message, or even more than one, as long as one understands what that *means*. And I would even agree with Carletto on the "value" of communicating sophisticated messages in sophisticated ways: the more complex the play, the more useful it is. The only delusion here may be the realist hypothesis in the background: the idea that having value amounts to possessing a thing called "value," which leads its impassible existence in a transcendent world, and to which we try to get closer through contact with the things that *have it*. To have value for me is just to fulfil a function relative to given ends, first of all survival. But psychologically it's quite difficult to accept this position, and hence a certain amount of realist delusion may be necessary.

B: Our souls are too weak?

A: I'd rather say that they're too much *our own*.

B: What do you mean?

A: A long time ago I saw the movie *The Hellstrom Chronicle*, a sort of documentary on the theme: how and why insects will defeat us and dominate the planet. I was highly impressed by a scene in that movie, which acquired for me a great symbolic value. We see a horde of ferocious ants launched on a mad expedition during which they literally devour any living being they run into. Nothing can stop the horde: when they reach a stream, a few individuals form a bridge by clinging to one another, and the others use the bridge to cross the stream. The bridge-ants are eventually swept away by the current, but by then the rest of the horde is already on the other side. Every time I think of this scene I can't help asking: who among us would be willing to be part of the bridge?

B: That's why insects will win.

A: Right! Indeed this scene illustrated convincingly one of the movie's main themes: man needs personal salvation, he must believe that what he does somehow will help *him*. Therefore, I would add now, nature often has no alternative to deceiving him.

B: Letting him believe that he's obtaining direct and private advantages when in fact only the species profits from the situation?

A: Yes. For instance, letting him believe that he's getting hold of some Platonic entity hidden behind the *Resurrection*, whereas what's involved in the *Resurrection* is the old, precious game of finding one's way in a maze.

C: Listening to you, it would seem that not only can there be no artistic progress but there cannot even be any artistic development. It's always the same old game, you say; are you claiming that the *Resurrection* is no better than the graffiti drawn by primitive people in their caves?

A: No. I only want to deny that such value judgments can be given in an absolute way—understanding this word literally, as *absolutus, disconnected*, independent of any perspective. The history of a development, of a progress, or a regress, is always written *by* someone *for* someone—people who, because they are what they are, can only enjoy certain things, can *no longer* enjoy others, and possibly can *go back* to enjoying yet others.

C: In conclusion, then, anything goes. "What we are" will be transformed according to blind, fortuitous laws, and our aesthetic experiences will follow passively, forever repeating the ineluctable cycle of the reel in *Beyond the Pleasure Principle* that first eludes us and then is found again.

B: All rationalized by a "perspectival"—or maybe we should say, more honestly, partisan—history that makes us regard as necessary and universal what is only the fruit of our conditioning. In other words: beauty is in the eye of the beholder.

A: Though formulated with little sympathy, your analysis is substantially correct; at most, it's the conclusion that puzzles me. I'm not sure that anything goes, that what we are can be extended in any direction, widened indefinitely. I believe that modifications and extensions are only possible within a certain range; beyond that, the equilibrium is broken and change becomes qualitative, not just quantitative. Just as a man thirty feet or an inch tall would be crushed by the air pressure or prey to incurable articular diseases, a human society subject to demands *too* differ-

ent from those faced so far should probably call it quits and pass the baton
to another form of life.

B: Here you go again with your typical catastrophic attitude. No wonder
you liked *The Hellstrom Chronicle* so much. But these jeremiads of yours
seem to have little to do with aesthetics, and your insistence on bringing
them out, one way or another . . .

A: They do have something to do with aesthetics, don't worry. And my
attitude is not catastrophic, at least not in the sense of something vaguely
concerned with the future. It's a concrete preoccupation, originating from
an examination of our *present* state.

C: The enemy is already among us!

A: In a way.

B: I wouldn't miss this for the world: Angelo worried about something
concrete. Though I suspect that it's only "concrete" for him.

A: For the moment, maybe. But I wouldn't want to see it become
tragically concrete for everyone.

B: Do enlighten us, so we'll be able to avoid this Armageddon.

A: See, it's precisely a question of size. For the play I'm talking
about to be practiced and enjoyed, it must fall within definite perceptual
limits, established by our sensory apparatus. For example, we can't see
things that are too small or too big, and hence we can get involved
with a given style of expression, and gradually learn to understand it
and master it, taking pleasure in this activity, only if the elements of
the style are accessible to us, if they don't exceed our limits in one
direction or the other.

B: I don't understand yet.

A: Take a medieval town, and suppose you enter it as a stranger.
You look around and see palaces and churches, columns and friezes.
You go into those palaces and churches and discover statues, busts,
altar-pieces, and frescoes. You have an extraordinary diversity available,
an enormous "space" for your perceptual adventures, and—what matters most—such diversity and availability are both integrated in everyday
environments and made to your scale—that is, the objects instantiating
them can be not only analyzed but also *synthesized* by your eye, with
no artificial help. But now suppose you enter a contemporary city,
indeed one of the most extreme expressions of the "contemporary
spirit," say Los Angeles, or Houston. What do you find? Nameless
cubes, one after the other, all looking identical; straight, wide streets,
crossing at right angles; periodic appearances of the same gas stations,
the same supermarkets, the same department stores. Any part of town

is like any other, and hence none is recognizable; to be in one place is just like being in another, *any* other. What's recognizable, the "artistic" product, is hidden in some of those cubes, under the airtight protection of a thousand security systems and, above all, entirely safe from everyday life—which reproduces itself in a sort of modular paroxysm or obtuse metastasis.

C: You seem to be exaggerating. Do you mean to imply, with this obvious reference to cancer, that contemporary urban development has no structure, that it communicates no message?

A: No, that is not my point. The message is there: what I'm asking is whether we can read it. If you study a contemporary city with aerial photographs, you can see its structure, but when you're in the city, the structure is too big and you lose sight of it.

C: Well, then one must avail oneself of the proper tools to recover it. You just mentioned aerial photographs.

A: The structure presented by a photograph is a pattern on paper. And you don't live on paper; at most, a *representation* of you does. You might need—this is my tragic worry—something more corporeal, a more immediately perceptible message, a more sensual and physical "play," less abstract, less "by proxy." Besides, not everyone can afford to familiarize himself with patterns on paper and photographs: most of us have something else to do, and if while doing it we face only nameless cubes and straight streets, our inventiveness and willingness to take risks are subject to a constant degradation, an implacable decline.

B: To Big Brother's advantage?

A: Maybe. But, most important, to the disadvantage of the species' adaptive capacity.

B: But what if things turned out for the better? What if we became more like ants, and each of us fulfilled his little task in a compartmentalized structure, without even asking what the sense of the whole thing is?

A: Who knows? You may be right.

C: What a gain! I don't care to be an ant. What's the difference between letting ants win and becoming ants ourselves? Ants as a species would have won anyway. But I want man to win, the *project* man, the *idea* man, and I'll continue to fight for that, to invent absurdities and rediscover ancient proposals—or maybe combine the two as I'm trying to do here.

B: Yes, indeed, *what* are you trying to do here?

C: You really want to know, eh? Well, then I'll tell you; I think you've earned it . . .